Additional Testimonials:

"I consider Ryan Sauers more than a thought leader. That term gets thrown around too much these days. Ryan has gone deeper. He has dedicated his life to marrying thought with practice. His book is a reflection of his desire to bundle ideas with practice. Rather than simply lecture us about the culture of sales that must run through every department, Ryan offers real world ideas for the graphics industry that can be put into practice immediately. Ryan is a sincerely positive influence on everyone he comes in contact with. Subsequently, his new book connects with us all."

— Mark Potter, Publisher, *CANVAS* magazine

"If you are looking for a great read that bridges the world of traditional and new media, this is the book. Although we have new ways to communicate, the human element is not lost. Ryan's book will tell you how to sell in the new media world of digital while maintaining the importance of being human and selling to others."

— Amy Howell, CEO & Founder,
Howell Marketing Strategies, LLC

"Whether you're a librarian, marketing manager, or basketball coach, you're in sales. As Ryan Sauers so effectively demonstrates in this book, embracing the 'everyone is in sales' philosophy will give you a much better chance of successfully communicating with your audience, no matter what you want them to hear and understand."

— Kent Huffman, Co-Publisher of
Social Media Marketing Magazine

Everyone is in SALES

in

From the
Ball Field
to the
Boardroom

RYAN T. SAUERS

Everyone Is in Sales

ISBN: 978-0615567280

Library of Congress Control Number: 2011943951

CONTENTS

Dedication

This book is dedicated to the good Lord above who gave
me the strength, wisdom and energy to write this book.
I also dedicate this book to my wonderful wife Lara and
three terrific daughters Kelsey, McKenna and Brooke.
Your support, understanding, patience, love, and belief in
me means more than you will ever know.

Acknowledgements

Wow, how can I begin to acknowledge all of the great people who have played a role in my writing this book? There are so many of you that I cannot possibly do this justice—but I will try. Writing this book has been a longtime goal of mine, and although it has been a large undertaking, it is one that I have greatly enjoyed.

First, let me thank all of my family and friends. I cannot begin to name each one of you, but please know how important you are to me. You have provided me encouragement in this process. You have listened to my stories and the "ups and downs" of writing a book. You know who you are, and so do I—and I appreciate you more than you will ever know. So, thanks for encouraging me to go for it and for your unconditional support and belief in this concept.

Secondly, I want to thank the persons whom I interviewed for this book. Each of you provided great insights that helped me further develop the *Everyone Is in Sales* philosophy. In addition, I want to thank each person who took time to write a testimonial or foreword for the book. Each one of you is special to me. I greatly appreciate your kind words and support of both me and this book.

Third, there are a few people I must name who have played an instrumental role in day-to-day logistics of getting this book done. To Steve Peterson, my cover designer, thank you for your creative work on this cover. To Lorrie Bryan, my editor, thank you for your attention to detail, being wonderful to work with, and making this book the best it could be. To Elsie Olson, my graphic designer, you have done a superb job in making this book flow and giving this your all.

Finally, I want to acknowledge and thank Sherry Smith. You have played an instrumental role in making this book a reality. Thank you for your patience, friendship, and hard work. Sherry, without your help, this book might not have happened—you were the first person to embrace the *Everyone Is in Sales* philosophy, and you helped motivate me to write it. I sincerely thank you for all of your tireless work in helping me put this book together.

Ryan T. Sauers, Author
Everyone Is in Sales

Foreword

One of the things that distinguishes me in the world of social media marketing is that I am old...at least old enough to remember how things used to be before we were digitally immersed, consumed, and tethered.

I was in sales before Facebook...before email...even before computers. Not that long ago, relationships were built through a firm handshake, a trusting friendship, a relationship built on mutually-shared experiences and trust.

And then, sometime in the late 1990s, your company probably took all its order forms, sales brochures, and customer service policies to a strange person called a web developer and said, "turn this into a website."

We could have hardly realized it at the time but we were creating a layer of digital distance between ourselves and our customers that would only become more tangled as layer upon layer of technology was wedged between us. And it was a one-way ticket.

Sure, it was efficient. Administrative costs went down and customers had the convenience of placing orders through our new machines at any time of day or night.

And yet, something was missing. The soul of business was reduced to computer keystrokes.

When writing my book *Return on Influence*, I asked the celebrated author and speaker Dr. Robert Cialdini what he thought it took to stand out in this increasingly dense and competitive digital world. His reply was simple. "Be more human."

Doesn't that seem ironic?

Being human, simply being ourselves, can create competitive advantage!

I think that is the heart of this book. Ryan Sauers realizes that behind the Twitter avatars and Facebook updates, the text messages and the Skype conferences, people are the same. They still want to be acknowledged. They want to be heard. They want to cut through that digital distance and get to know you as a person. They seek real communications.

It is time to unleash the human potential in both your organization and every part of your life. Everyone should contribute. Everyone is part of the customer equation. Everyone should be in sales.

And it's time to have Ryan show us how.

Let's begin.

> Mark W. Schaefer
> Rutgers University faculty
> Author of *The Tao of Twitter* and *Return on Influence*

SECTION I

Thinking of Sales in a New Way

CHAPTER 1

We Are All in Sales?

"Did you say I was in sales? Wait, not me. Never! I can't stand salespersons. They are pushy and always try to convince me to buy things I don't need. So, please don't compare me to a salesperson. That's not me—I am not in sales!

If that is what you are thinking, you are in for a good read. This book works to dispel such thought processes, and this is one of the many reasons that *Everyone Is in Sales* has been written. As you will see, this book explains sales so that people can see the entire process in a new way.

So, why does our society generally view salespersons in a negative manner? Why does the word *sales* carry negative connotations? Does it conjure up memories of the stereotypical used car salesman who refused to let us off the car lot? Or, do we recall the telemarketing lady that rudely interrupted our dinner?

Perhaps we think that *being in sales* means a person talks a lot or has the "gift of gab." Or, maybe we think of sales as someone who "pounds the pavement," going door to door and makes tons of cold calls to earn a living. Maybe we hear the word *sales* and think of a gimmicky salesperson who is trying to pull a fast one on us to get a sale. Nobody wants to be thought of as "that salesperson." You know the ones I am talking about—the guy with the power handshake, the lady who repeatedly says your name, the man with the clip-on tie and heavy cologne, or the woman who talks over you. So maybe this is why so many of us argue that we are not in sales. Many of us act as if being in sales is a curse.

> *Why, then, do organizations and individuals fight the notion that everyone is in sales?*

Here are the facts. While most of the worlds's employees and workers do not have the word *sales* mentioned anywhere in their job description or title—they are in sales. Why, then, do organizations and individuals fight the notion that everyone is in sales? One reason and one reason alone; our definition of *sales* is fundamentally flawed.

> *When Ken says to Amy, "I feel a connection between us...Let's get together for coffee and talk sometime," is Ken in sales?*

Well, what is he really up to? He wants Amy to get the message that he might be interested in her. He is also suggesting that she could be interested in him. Then he is making a casual offer to get together, but makes it tentative by using the word *sometime.*

This communications encounter between Ken and Amy was not sales as we normally think of it but guess what—it was indeed sales.

For those who are not trained in traditional sales—such as the computer, operations or financial types—this looks like a guy just trying to get a date, right? OK, let's consider another scenario.

Jennifer, the accounting manager, has just been assigned a time-intensive, special budgeting project. It is June 30th and the director of finance, needs the report on July 5th. The three accountants in her department need to work on the project, but they are expecting to spend a long holiday weekend at home with their families.

Jennifer calls a meeting. She begins by explaining that there is a special project that will produce a report that could be instrumental in determining the company's future. She explains that those who work on the project will be in a unique position to see the possibilities for the company expansion, which could mean greater opportunities for their own personal advancement. She then asks the three employees to work over the holiday weekend to make this happen, and, as a bonus, earn a few comp days. Jennifer finishes by thanking them in advance for their help and commitment.

Again, if you have experience in being a traditional salesperson, you likely recognize that Jennifer has positioned the project in a better way. She communicated in a manner that explained the benefit the accountants would receive through their participation. She offers additional incentive to work (comp time), and then assumes their agreement by thanking them in advance. Wow, this is a classic sales presentation model, and guess what? It comes from a "non-salesperson" who works in accounting.

If you are an accountant you may simply see this scenario as one where the boss is making you work over the holiday. In reality, even though Jennifer is not a salesperson in the traditional sense of the word, she clearly had to sell her team on the project, right? Without their buy in she would have a hard time achieving the task at hand. So could it be that an accounting person was selling her position to her employees? Absolutely!

OK, in the event I have yet to make you consider the fact that *Everyone Is in Sales*, here's one more scenario for you to consider.

> *Your 4-year-old is determined to get a candy bar before you get out of the grocery store. You are determined that he is not getting any candy. In addition, you don't want a scene at the checkout line.*

> *In the freezer section, as you pick up the last thing on your list, you turn to your son and say, "I can't wait to get home and slice some of these pretty apples for a snack. How about we make some special dipping sauce for them? You can help me pick out the best apples and mix up the sauce. Won't that be fun? Let's hurry and check out so we can get home fast. OK?"*

If you were enthusiastic enough, your son is now focused on the snack and the fun he will enjoy at home. He has been distracted from his original goal of getting a candy bar, and the entire situation has been reframed.

So, was sales involved? With a 4-year-old? You bet there was. You had a different objective than your son. You offered an alternative possibility, made it sound attractive, and suggested a quick exit from the store to start having fun. My friends, that *is* sales.

If all of these scenarios are sales, and they are, then keep reading as I explain ways to see sales in new and unique ways in this book. You will be glad you did.

This book is targeted at those who do not work in traditional sales; yet will be quite relevant to "traditional salespersons" too. My goal was to write a book that really explained sales in a new way to people who have not spent much or any time in a traditional sales position.

Your learning curve will be quicker than those in traditional sales who will have to rethink and relearn the way they do things.

Everyone Is in Sales is an overall mindset. It provides people a way to think about sales in a new way. My objective is for you to see the word *sales* as pleasant, doable and understandable. And again, this book will help traditionally trained salespersons think and grow in new ways as well.

It is time to create a paradigm shift in your thinking regarding the word *sales. Everyone Is in Sales,* because we all have information that we need to share with others. If something is important to you, don't you try to express it to another person so that they understand you? Our need to share and be understood are fundamental parts of the human condition. You may not think of this as sales but it is.

> **When a problem develops and you have to communicate the issue with someone else, that is sales.**

If you are in accounting you have to deal with people to do your job, get money collected, and close the monthly books. Therefore, you are in sales, because without the help of others you will not get your job done. How about the operations guy who says he is not in sales? Well, when the machine goes down, and he needs someone to come in for an immediate repair job, you better believe he is in sales mode. What about talking to your boss during your annual review or talking to your child's principal about their performance in school? You are *selling* your case, right?

When a problem develops and you have to communicate the issue with someone else, that is sales. Truly it is all about sales, but just a different type of sales. So, if you seek to understand a new way to think about sales this is the book for you. If you desire to learn innovative methods that will create more personal and company success for you, do not put this book down. (A little *sales* there, huh?)

And finally, if you are seeking a more meaningful way to achieve your communications goals while feeling validated that what you do is important, acceptable and rational, let's get started. Things can be easier and more satisfying. I promise.

As you read this book, I will show you ways to embrace the notion of sales as a positive, useful way to improve your human interactions in all aspects of your life. We will reframe the concept of sales to encompass all of our purposeful communications.

The end goal is to help you sell (communicate) your ideas, positions, desires, feelings and, yes, products or services to others you encounter in a mutually beneficial manner. If you can do this, success is yours as an individual, a team, a family, or an organization. If you can improve your interaction with others, you will be a better friend, spouse, parent, boss, and, yes, salesperson.

The organizations that adopt the *Everyone Is in Sales* philosophy will be the leaders now and in the years ahead. Such organizations will enhance their bottom line and provide top-line value for their customers. Everyone wins. Everyone is happy. *Everyone Is in Sales.*

So, let's re-evaluate our assumptions, broaden our visions, and learn new ways to accomplish our sales/communication objectives. This book will cover time-tested communications truths and share what this means to us in our rapidly changing world. The end result is that you will be inspired to change and use these new tools to achieve greater success. So, jump on board, and buckle your seatbelts for an exciting journey. You will be glad you did. Wait...I think I might have just "sold you" on continuing to read this book. You get the idea.

CHAPTER 2

Reframing of Sales to Communications

The journey we are on is different. It is unique. It will be informative. And, did I mention that it will be fun? When you embrace the *Everyone Is in Sales* philosophy the term *sales* becomes different from traditional definitions of the word. When you begin thinking in this new way, you become part of a select group that recognizes sales as a form of communications. So, simply said, this book is about communications.

This means *communications plural*. (Yes, with an "s" at the end.) Communications is a two-way process that is focused on having conversations with others. It is about talking with people; not at them. At times, I will use the words *sales* and *communications* interchangeably, but the idea is still the same. So, begin to reframe your thinking so you can see that sales is a form of communications. Now, if I were to ask you, "Are you in communications?" Most people would quickly say "yes." Right?

Before we go further, however, let me remind you how traditional sales is generally defined and discussed. First, it focuses on the concept of moving goods and services. We think of a salesperson as the one who persuades a customer to buy such goods and/or services.

Salespersons are often thought of as the people that make cold calls, have nice expense accounts, and attend networking events. The word *sales*, until now, has been reserved for those people whose job it is to, well...*sell*. As an example, think of a person whose full-time job it is to "wine and dine" clients to make them feel appreciated and keep the client's business. This is the classic example of a salesperson.

> *If you embrace this new way of thinking, you become part of a select group that recognizes sales as a form of communications.*

The traditional idea of sales often involves a salesperson's being taught persuasive techniques learned in sales seminars and training sessions. Techniques include: using a power handshake, maintaining excessive eye contact, repeating someone's name in a deliberate manner, or body mirroring. Uhhh... in my estimation these shortcuts, while they can be effective for short-term results, need to go away. They are just that; shortcuts and gimmicks. If you get nothing else from this book, please ditch these types of memorized and robotic behaviors.

Many traditional salespersons seem to guard the concept of sales as if it were a secret only they know the answer to. The people in the organization (who are "not" in sales) seem to validate this by thinking salespersons, in the traditional sense of the word, have some magical formula only available to them to obtain and keep business. Sorry, but this is not true, and secondly, this is not what this book is about. It is, however, about tearing down the curtain so we can all see our role in sales—in every part of our life—in a new way.

So, in the past when I asked some colleagues if they were in sales, they generally agreed that every salesperson was in sales, but stated if you were not in "traditional sales" then you were not in sales. Based on the typical definition of sales, this makes sense; however, this traditional understanding of sales is limited. It only considers a small portion of the sales activities that take place every day. Sales is not an either/or option, but a must-do activity. Without good sales and communications in life you will be ineffective. It is that simple.

In our rapidly changing world, the time has come to reframe the concept of sales. It is now time to account for all of the "sales" that we are all involved in daily as a way of life, not a job description.

So, what is *sales* all about? It is quite simple. It is about being an honest, authentic and trustworthy communicator who establishes and maintains quality relationships with others. You see, if you do these things, you *are* in sales.

While doing research for this book, I spoke with a number of individuals, some of whom I first met through social media forums, where I posted this question: *Everyone Is in Sales*—agree or disagree, and why? Well I must have hit a hot button—the responses were incredible! I received hundreds upon hundreds of responses over a period of well over six months. I picked a handful of people from these forums and then conducted a phone interview with them in regard to the *Everyone Is in Sales* philosophy. To me, everything is about real world application.

After reflecting on my question, most people agreed with the concept that, yes, *Everyone Is in Sales.* In addition, the more they talked about the philosophy, the more they agreed with it. So let's hear some real-world feedback...

I spent meaningful time to talking to Rick Pranitis, owner of Tiger Cat Productions. Rick stated, "Everyone is selling whether they know it or not. The secret is in recognizing what is happening and then deciding how you use this information to achieve your objectives." Rick went on to state that the concept applies to his personal life as well. "I must constantly be aware of what I say, or do not say to others, and to what is going on around me. Just like in politics, there can be ramifications for anything I say." Rick, you are right on target, and I agree with you.

I had an enjoyable interview with Charles Duke who works in consulting. Charles commented, "We are all in sales, and this means we can't put on one face to one person and a different face to another person—such an approach would lack honesty and consistency. Communications are all about building relationships and trust. So, if you are above board and honest, you do not have to remember what you told people—whether online or offline." Well said, Charles, and I concur. This is one of the reasons I have written this book. Communications are about consistency, integrity and transparency and there is more to come on this later in the book.

Another interesting person I interviewed was John Patrick, an executive at Transworld Systems. John commented, "Sales is the transference of emotional conviction from one party to another and is not always about the exchange of money. In most encounters one party is thinking, while talking to the other party, what is in it for me? Thus, a person's ability to communicate well and 'sell' their position to the other party allows them to answer the what's-in-it for-me question."

I agree with John's assessment. Sales is not always about business or dollars, but people are always thinking, "What's in it for me?" I know that is hard to believe, but it is true. It is just how human beings are.

When interviewing Linda Lewis-McKee who works as a CPA at an accounting firm, I gained some new insights from a "non-traditional" salesperson. Linda comments, "There is an element of sales in everything I do—even in my field of accounting. It is not about a hard sale—where you push someone in a corner—but instead about a win-win sale where you try to meet another person's needs. The focus of our communications needs to be clear and consistent to get our message out, no matter what forum (online of offline) we are using." Linda is right on target.

What I want you to see through these interviews, is that this is not just a clever book title; this is instead a fundamental shift in the way we define sales. We are dealing with powerful human emotions, interactions and behaviors. This book has been developed through countless hours of research, real world experience, and interviews, to emphasize the importance of this concept.

My interview with Pat and Kevin Sinnott, co-owners of Sinnott Productions, was an enjoyable one. Pat shared, "Sales can be seen in how you treat a repair person that comes into your home. Do you make them feel important and valued? When you meet this basic human need, in most cases, the contractor will go above and beyond to help you." I agree with Pat. I always build a relationship with workers who come to my house. I ask them if they would like a soda or a drink of water. Why do I do this? Because I care about people, and they are working hard to help me. So this is one simple way to establish trust and show my appreciation.

The interview that I had with Mike Feeley, VP in the telecommunications industry, was insightful as well. He makes the point that, "You sell yourself, your car and home. Simply said, everyone is selling all the time. Sales is in large part like solving a puzzle." Mike is correct in his assessment, and this type of human *puzzle solving* that Mike refers to will be covered in the next chapter.

Finally, in my interview with Rebecca Lacy, president of Pinnacle Management Group, I was again provided with valuable insights. Rebecca said, "We are all in sales and must be conscious of how we communicate as someone is always watching what we do. The key to good communications is trust. Communications are the foundation of everything we do." I agree with Rebecca's analysis, and this is the foundation of this book. Everyone is in sales, because everyone is in communications, whether they like it or not. Good communications are the foundation of what we do in all parts of life, and without such strong communications we do not have trust.

So, remember that we have expanded *sales* from its traditional and narrow minded definition to a modern and broader one. As we move on, we will look at various types of communications in both the online and offline world.

So you know, *offline* simply refers to any encounter that is not online. (You see, by defining this I am exhibiting good communications at work.) Also, you will read some examples of how some of my real world relationships (offline) initially began and formed through online mediums. You will also see real world examples of great, good and poor communications from real people and organizations (although I have changed the names for the sake of privacy.)

We will cover the types of communications strategies that you should use in selling your position through a number of scenarios. In addition, the book will explain why a solid communications plan is vital to selling your message. We will emphasize the importance of listening in the communications process. Now it is time to examine the 5 Why's Communications Model.

CHAPTER 3

The 5 Why's Communications Model

So, you may be thinking, "OK, sales *is* communications. I hear you, Ryan. But, what's the big deal?" Well, the reason it matters so much is that human beings, especially adults, have a hard time communicating with each other.

On the other hand, children are inclined to be more natural communicators. Have you ever seen a young child loudly and innocently ask his parent a question like, "What's that person wearing, Mommy?" I have seen this many times, and while the child is simply displaying his or her natural curiosity, the adult is mortified by the question.

You see, we have been conditioned through both nature and nurture to avoid saying certain things, and at other times, to respond in an almost robotic manner. So if someone asks—even when I am having a terrible day—"How are you today, Ryan?" I quickly say, "I am great…how are you?" So why do I do that? Why am I conditioned to automatically reply with that type of response? Why do I give an answer at all if I am having a horrible day—especially one that is not accurate? The questions go on.

This chapter takes a look at a model of decision making that I call *The 5 Why's Communications Model*. It is a method to ask questions in order to try and obtain real answers. The goal of continuing to ask another person *why* is to ultimately determine the root cause of a problem. With each *why* question, you should gain a deeper understanding of why another person feels the way he or she does.

Without understanding another person, their worldview and their truths, successful communications will not occur. People will never see things the same way, but this model helps us to understand the *why* behind a person's actions or behaviors. Stephen Covey says, "that human beings have the ability to choose their response to the world that occurs around them." By the way, the word responsibility means "response able."

> *Without understanding another person, their worldview and their truths, successful communications will not occur.*

In this book, I argue that we must become responsible and proactive communicators. We need to do this to sell our message in a way that meets the needs of the other person. The 5 Why's Communications Model provides a method and means to understand people in a new way. Here is an example of a conversation I recently had with my youngest daughter:

> *"Brooke, please buckle your seatbelt." (My 1st communications statement)*

> *"**Why**, Daddy?" (Note: Why #1)*

> *"Because I want you to be safe." (My #2 deeper rooted communications statement)*

> *"But, **why**, Daddy?" (Note: Why #2)*

14

"Because I don't want you to get hurt if I have to stop the car quickly." (#3 communications statement is even deeper)

*"But, **why** would that matter, Daddy?" (Note: Why #3)*

"Because you could get hurt bad if we had to suddenly stop, and you might end up in the hospital." (#4 communications statement even deeper)

*"But, **Why** is the hospital bad, Daddy?" (Note: Why #4)*

"I'm afraid it would be a scary experience for you, and it scares me to even think about it." (#5 communications statement—getting near core belief)

*"**Why** does it scare you to think about it, Daddy?" (Note: Why #5)*

"Because I love you so very much and always want to keep you safe." (#6 communications statement that—due to the 5 why questions—revealed the reason I wanted my daughter to buckle her seatbelt.)

I use this example because it is something we can all relate to. Moreover, it illustrates the new model of sales that we defined in the last chapter. In this scenario, I am selling my daughter on the importance of buckling her seatbelt. I avoided getting frustrated with her and instead was able to communicate with her in an effective manner about what I wanted her to do. However, for her communications needs to be met, she sought to understand the "why" behind my request.

Instead of simply saying, as we all often do, "…because I said so," I tried a different tact and it worked. So, even at a young age my daughter intuitively asked me five why-related questions, and in doing so uncovered why it was important to me that she buckle her seatbelt.

This is what effective two-way communications is all about. It is about having a conversation. It is about a dialogue. My daughter, Brooke, ended up having her needs met as she understood my goal was to protect her because I loved her. And I had my needs met as I was able to have Brooke do what I asked without yelling at her.

Again, unless we have been properly trained to uncover such bottom-line reasoning through a critical thinking process, adults tend to struggle in this area. We are apt to speak too much and not listen enough.

Here is another example to consider. My colleague Jeff, who works in traditional sales in a car dealership, shared a scenario that is applicable to this book.

A potential customer walked into the new car showroom early in his career. Jeff, who was a confident salesperson, approached the lady with a big smile.

He said, "Hey there, I'm Jeff and would love to help you. What's your name?

"Oh, I am Lisa."

Jeff said, "Welcome to Auto Center USA, Lisa. Anything I can help you find today?"

Lisa said, "No, not really. I am just looking."

Jeff asked, "Well when you are ready to buy, what type of car will you be looking for? This way I can give you some suggestions about what to look at."

Lisa said, "Thanks, but I am fine and just want to look around if that is OK?"

Jeff said, "You bet, Lisa. Here's my card. Please let me know if you have any questions."

With that Jeff evaluated the likelihood of the sale, walked away, and told his sales manager that Lisa was not a legitimate prospect. He then went to talk to another potential customer. Soon after this, Jeff and his sales colleagues worked with my consulting firm doing some sales and communications training.

Jeff told me this story during one of our training sessions, and I used it as a case study for the group to illustrate what could have been done differently. In other words, how could the communications have been better?

I praised Jeff for making a couple of attempts to engage Lisa and even going as far as trying to determine what her needs were. Moreover, I pointed out that Jeff and Lisa had communicated to some degree; however, I challenged Jeff regarding how deep his communications with Lisa had been.

For example, did he really know why she was there? The entire group decided that he did not and wanted to learn from this example. So, in the training we did a number of role playing exercises and I included the 5 Why's Communications Model as well. All of the salespersons walked away quite excited.

Jeff later shared with me how this training applied to his real world success six months later when a nearly identical situation developed. Watch closely as this time the results are different... and yes, I am a pleased consultant.

"Hey there I am Jeff. What brings you to Auto Center USA today?"

"Oh... I just wanted to look at some new cars"

Jeff replied, "Super and I am sorry but I didn't get your name..."

"I'm Mary."

17

*Jeff said, "Great, Mary. **Why** are you interested in looking at these cars?"*

Mary commented, "Well, I think they are well rated, and I like the looks of the new models."

*Jeff replied, "I agree they are nice, and they do get better gas mileage than last year's models, but **why** do they appeal to you?"*

Mary said, "That's a good question... I guess one big thing is the gas mileage. I drive 65 miles roundtrip to work every day. With gas prices being so high, it costs me a lot simply to get to and from work."

Jeff asked, "I hear you on that. Would you like to test drive the red model?"

Mary said, "No thanks, not today. I'm just looking."

*Jeff said, "Come on...**why** not drive it? There's no cost. At least this way—and you are already here—you will know if this is a car you would really be interested in."*

Mary commented, "Yes, that is true, but if I drive it, I might really like it."

*Jeff asked, "**Why** would that be a problem?"*

Mary said, "Because I don't have the money to buy it now."

*Jeff quickly asked "**Why** is that—as you could save so much money on gas alone?"*

Mary shared, "This may be true, but my father taught me that I should have some money saved up before I buy a car. Financing costs too much in interest."

Jeff, stated, "Seems like you have a smart dad. If you could buy this car, save money on gas, be in a newer car and make reasonable payments—that included less than 2 percent interest—do you think your dad might approve?"

Mary exclaimed, "Did you say only 2 percent interest? I'd save that much in gas alone… let's do that test drive."

What's the difference between the two conversations? In the second scenario, Jeff approached the sales encounter in a different way. He did not look at Mary as a "deal to be closed" like he had done with Lisa.

Instead he looked at Mary as person who he needed to communicate effectively with to determine if he could meet her transportation needs. Furthermore, he used the 5 Why's Communications Model to find out the core reason Mary was looking at cars—which he never discovered from Lisa.

This time he was properly trained. In the second story, Jeff ultimately sold the car because he did not make assumptions. He asked good questions and successfully communicated with Mary. Her needs were met in a manner that made her feel comfortable. She was not being "talked to" she was being "talked with" which is a big difference.

Mary wanted a new car. She needed a new car. It made financial sense to get a new car. She had the income for a new car. But, she was holding back because her father had taught her long ago that it was not good to finance things that cost a lot of money in interest.

In the first scenario it appeared that Lisa didn't really want a new car and was just killing time. So, Jeff dismissed her as a buyer and moved on to another person in the showroom. The problem, which we discussed in the training, was he never took time to fully understand Lisa's reasons for being there. Notice that he never asked any "why" questions.

In the second scenario, Jeff communicated in an effective manner. Mary trusted him, and in a very non-threatening way, he was able to uncover Mary's motivations. The depth of communications made all the difference. Until we truly know how to communicate with other people in depth, real communications do not occur. When we embrace the *Everyone Is in Sales* philosophy we are aware that such situations occur all the time and in every aspect of our lives.

Why is deeper communications important?

It's important because all human beings have an innate desire to be appreciated, valued and understood. All individuals have their own biases, beliefs and truths by which they make sense of the world around them.

Why does this matter?

It matters because our frame of reference can be thought of as our worldview. It is why we think the way we do. It is also why we often jump to conclusions. It is the "truth" we carry around with us and what we rely on in making decisions about people and situations.

Why does that affect my communications with others?

It affects you when you are trying to interact with another person, whether on a personal or professional level. If you do not understand the worldview or truth that is so real to the person you are communicating with, you are apt to have misunderstandings or disagreements in your discussions.

Why is that?

The outcome of any human interaction is based on deeply held opinions that determine the response of the people with whom you interact. For a person to feel comfortable hearing what you have to say, it is imperative that trust first be established. Once this trust is established then a relationship can be built.

So, **why** is that important?

It is critically important if you are in sales, as we all are, because you can only effectively persuade or motivate another person if you truly understand why they feel the way they do.

The 5 Why's Communications Model is effective and something you can use in every aspect of your life. It will make you a better communicator. So, we have reframed the word *sales* to *communications*. So the next question is what does communications mean?

CHAPTER 4

Sales Is All About Communications

I frequently say life is all about communications. Notice I say *communications*, with an "s" at the end, and not *communication*. Most of us use the two words interchangeably and see little difference between the two. I have an undergraduate degree in the discipline and am not sure, without looking, whether it says Communication or Communications. So we can truly embrace the *Everyone Is in Sales* philosophy, in this chapter I will explain the differences between the two words.

> ***Communications are about collaboration, community and connection.***

So, what difference does one little "s" make? Well, a lot. The word *communication* is singular in nature. It implies one-way communication. In contrast, the word *communications* is plural and two-way in nature. *Communications*, in any form, require human interaction with at least two people. *Communications* are about collaboration, community and connection. To help explain

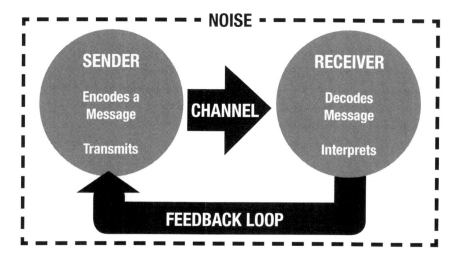

this idea, here is a simple model (looks quite basic in today's world) that shows the *communications* cycle.

As you can see the basic idea of the communications model (in its simplest form) is comprised of a *sender* and a *receiver*. The *sender* is the one who creates a message and is trying to transmit it to the *receiver*. Notice the word *channel* in the middle. This is the medium the sender chooses to send their message to the receiver. The choice of channel has always been important, but it even more esssential today.

(Examples could include: email, calling on the phone, text messaging, tweeting, or via facebook.) There are many channels to choose from, and as a side note, always remember to pick the medium that is most appropriate for what you seek to accomplish. For example, email may work OK if you are affirming and praising an employee, but is not a good choice for reprimanding or criticizing an employee.

While I am at it (hint-hint), almost all of our newer communication channels—see the model later in this chapter—that are not via phone or in person backfire when the communications are dealing with a negative subject. Just trust me…that all the *LOL*,

J/K and *smiley faces* in the world do not make up for human tone, expression and other non-verbal cues.

OK, back to the communications model. So we have a *sender* who has picked the channel through which to communicate a message to a *receiver*. The *receiver* is the person who must understand and interpret the message from the sender. If the message is correctly understood, then successful communications have occurred.

How does the sender know that? Through the feedback received from the receiver as per the feedback loop above. Good feedback, neutral feedback, negative feedback, or no feedback are all important to consider in deciding if the sender's message has been successfully transmitted to the receiver. Later in this book, we have a chapter on 5 C's to consider in your communications. It will help you ensure your message is on target.

However, many times good communications do not occur. Why? Let's look at the model again. We have so much noise around us, that it is hard to find a quiet place to think these days. Thus, it is easy for the sender's message to get lost, missed or confused. You get the idea.

So, remember that communications (plural) is always a two-or-more person endeavor, which is the focus of this book. Let's take a look at a hypothetical example in the conversation below:

> *Mr. Anders needs to purchase a new computer. His only need for the computer is to do basic word processing and to email his friends. Jack, who works in traditional sales as a sales associate for Computer Etc., approaches Mr. Anders and goes into the typical "fast pitched and non-listening" sales mode.*
>
> *Jack says, "Hey there, how can I help you today? We have a great sale going on our top-of-the-line*

computer. Man, it is awesome and can do anything you need."

Ryan's Remarks: Notice the traditional sales pitch that Jack is giving. It is based on what Jack wants to talk about, is excited about, and what his company is trying to push. He asks nothing about Mr. Anders' (the customer's) needs. (remember the 5 Why's Communications Model) I do not see many deep fact finding and *why* related questions here.

"Well," says Mr. Anders, "I just need a basic computer to replace my old desk top model. What options do you have for that?"

"Let me show you what this new computer will do for you," says Jack. "You can stream movies, use your social media tools; and video chat with your friends and family. Again, it is on sale, and it is our top-of-the-line model."

Ryan's Remarks: Notice, another rookie communications mistake. Jack did not listen to one thing Mr. Anders said. And, if he did listen he certainly gave no feedback to that effect. Mr. Anders had some basic computer needs, which he had not even shared with Jack yet, but Jack continued talking about other things that were not even relevant to Mr. Anders buying decision. In addition, Jack uses the gimmicky phrase our "top-of-the-line" model.

"Well, that sounds nice, but all I ever do is write our neighborhood newsletter and send a few emails," replies Mr. Anders.

"Sure, no worries....It can do those things too if you purchase the publishing and email software with it. I will see if we have one in stock so you can take it home today," Jack says.

Ryan's Remarks: Jack made a number of communications mistakes. Number one, he came across as the prototypical pushy salesperson that we described early in this book. Nobody wants to be *that* salesperson. Also, it is clear that Jack is not interested in solving Mr. Anders needs but is instead focused on pushing the computer he wants to sell.

We end this story as Jack starts looking up the computer that he (not the customer) keeps talking about. In this one encounter, Jack assumes a lot, does not listen, gives "half answers" and seems to know more than his customer. The *Everyone Is in Sales* philosophy, which centers on solid communications, does not occur here.

Although, there is two-way "talking" taking place, they are not communicating. Without good feedback to ensure a message is understood by the receiver, the sender cannot assume that the message has been understood. I am sure you can relate to this example.

What if you are talking to a friend about one thing, but they keep cutting you off and not hearing you out. You try to convey a point, it is misunderstood, and the frustration begins to mount. Do you know where most disagreements, fights, and standoffs come from? OK, I am throwing you an easy lob pitch to knock it out of the park. Yes, most of these situations come from ineffective communications.

Successful communications only occur when what is being expressed by the sender is clearly understood by the receiver. If someone says they are a good communicator, yet others cannot understand what the individual has expressed, the fact of the matter is, that person is not an adept communicator and has failed in his or her communications attempt.

Here is another example. Think of a time when you were negotiating with someone. In many cases, one side tends to think their point of view is "right" and the other's vantage point is "wrong." A recent political debate provides a great example of this. I watched as the two politicians tried to communicate what needed to be done to create new jobs. Their conversation is captured below. By the way—before they began the debate—they both told everyone their goal was to truly listen to each other.

> *The Republican candidate stated, "We need to cut taxes so that our local businesses will have more money to hire additional people."*

> *The Democratic candidate replied, "Absolutely not. We need to raise taxes so that we can create real jobs by putting people to work on our highway systems."*

> *"You are wrong", declared the Republican. "Government cannot create jobs effectively."*

> *"No, you are wrong and I am right. Only government can be counted on to make the jobs happen. We can't trust business to do it," argued the Democrat.*

OK, I know that some of you don't care for politics being brought into this book; however, I am simply using their debate to make a point. And for the record, I am not endorsing any political point of view in this book unless of course…it will allow me to sell more copies of this book. (Did I mention that *Everyone Is in Sales?*) All kidding aside, if we take a step back and think about it, neither of these two politicians had all the answers.

Instead of hearing each other out as promised, they resorted to an ineffective communications cycle that was about *Either/ Or* instead of *Both/And*. *Either/Or* thinking means that you have to choose one option or the other, and effectively means there is no room for compromise. *Both/And* thinking allows for middle ground and additional options to be considered. We all know that many times the best answer is in the middle. In addition, neither side is ever 100 percent right or wrong in such arguments.

However, if neither side will acknowledge that there is room for middle ground and that a compromise between two hardline positions is possible, there is no chance for two-way communications to occur. People, especially in times of great emotion, become so focused on being "right" that they fail to listen to the other side long enough to even ponder their position. Such behavior causes communications to break down.

Stephen Covey states, "seek first to understand then be understood," which is a principle of great interpersonal communication."I could not agree more—except for the fact that there was no "s" at the end of the word communication in the previous sentence.

So, again the importance of embracing the *Everyone Is in Sales* mindset is similar to that of seeking first to understand and then to be understood. Both allow for human needs to be met so that true two-way communications and dialogue can occur.

You are reading this book right now. If you do not understand what I am saying, then good communications are not taking place. Maybe I could have written more clearly or used more examples? Or, maybe you could have taken time to re-read parts to truly embrace the concepts. The possibilities are endless.

When a lack of communications occurs, in any aspect of life, negative actions tend to follow. In many cases, this is because one side is not actively listening to the other. Here is one I heard in my house a few months back.

"Kelsey, please get the cat some more food and water," asked my wife, Lara, for the fifth time.

"Yeah sure, Mom," replied Kelsey as she went back to texting her friend.

No effective communications have occurred here. All that happened is both parties said words, heard words and are likely frustrated with the other. However, no listening took place.

One-way and stifled communication instead of healthy and free flowing communications occur when people in the conversation are focused on what they are going to say next. This means you have the notion that whatever brilliant concept you are going to say next is more important than what the other person is currently saying.

There is a big difference between "kind of listening" and being an engaged and active listener. The person who does the latter embraces the *Everyone Is in Sales* mentality. The active listener is present in the moment.

In both of the aforementioned situations, the skill of listening is not present. Great communicators are superb listeners. The two go hand in hand. Listening skills, as they relate to the communications process, are many times overlooked. However as the old saying goes, "we have two ears and one mouth for a reason." So, again, listening skills are very powerful. I work on mine every day...and it is hard work.

But, wow, do I enjoy being around great listeners. Why? They make me feel valued. They make me feel important and that what I say matters. Sometimes they say very little, but I know they are totally focused on what I am sharing. Some of my favorite people in this world fall into this category of great listeners, and they model great communications, not by how much they say but by how well they listen.

When successful communications occur, all parties can easily explain what has been communicated. This communications process is vital in every aspect of life. We all know in our everyday world there are too many times when we say something, but the other party hears it in a completely different way. Remember this saying as you embrace the *Everyone Is in Sales* mentality: *Misunderstandings = Miscommunications*.

So here is a challenge. Take some time and watch carefully, as things happen around you in the coming weeks, and see how many problems develop from one person or group not understanding or communicating successfully with the other.

Here's an example from a sales meeting that one of my colleagues attended.

Art, the sales manager, starts the meeting with, "Well team, we are almost at the end of the month and it looks like we are behind the curve on our sales goals. Let's take a few minutes to review the benefits of our newest product offering so we can get more customers to buy it."

Lynn, the top sales representative, hears, "Really? Does he think I'm too dumb to remember what we've already gone over ten times?

Phil, an average performing sales representative, hears, "Good idea. It never hurts to reinforce and practice the sales benefits."

John, the weakest sales producer hears, "Oh no, he is going to fire me because he listened in on that call yesterday where I gave up too fast."

Art believes he is simply encouraging his salespersons by providing additional reminders and training. None of the parties in the room hear the same thing. Yes, the same words were said by Art...but were interpreted differently by each of the three individuals. Always, remember that everyone comes to each situation in life with a different frame of reference. In this example, the strong performer is insulted, the average performer agrees, and the weak performer is scared.

So, what is the communications problem? Perhaps Art could have said that he just wanted to help each perform their best by providing some reinforcement training. However, even the different word choice would not change the interpretation of the message since each of his representatives—approached the meeting with different mindsets.

We all communicate in different ways and have preferences for the types of communications we like the best. If you are an enthusiastic "big picture" type who loves to share ideas, you are most likely to enjoy communicating with others who have the same style.

Why? You think in a similar manner, and it is easy to get your message across.

On the other hand, if you prefer to discuss one issue at a time in a more sequential manner, you will be more comfortable communicating with a "just the facts" type person.

In a selling situation, whether it is a coach motivating a player or the sales manager trying to convince a buyer to sign a contract, you will be far more successful if you and your listener have similar communications styles.

Simone, a friend of mine, is a vivacious young woman pitching a new advertising campaign to the CFO of a large Rhode Island accounting firm. Ronald, the CFO, is an intense, bottom line and detail oriented executive. Since the campaign will require a significant financial investment, he is the ultimate decision maker.

"Ronald, It's great to have a chance to show you this exciting new campaign. It will make your firm the best known name in the industry," Simone begins.

"Let me show you how we will promote your brand to so many businesses that need your services. Look at the video I've prepared, and it will show you how social media will help you grow... "

After the video, Ronald begins, "OK, Simone, that is a neat video but what specific markets are you targeting, what it the time needed to use social media, and what will the per customer acquisition cost likely be? "

Simone is communicating based on her preferred style, and Ronald, with his most comfortable style. Since they are so different, this results in missed communications. Simone is left to wonder why Ronald can't see how bold and powerful this campaign can be, and Ronald is trying to understand why he should even consider Simone's proposal. Guess what—the deal did not happen.

So, we see various people prefer to communicate in different ways. We also know that it is always easier to communicate with people who share the same "default" style that we do.

Does this mean we are doomed to a world of miscommunications when talking to those with different styles? Does it mean we can only successfully communicate with people who have styles similar to our own? Of course not. Good, clear, understandable communications occur every day between people who have a wide variety of communications styles.

Don't most of us try and "read" the other person we are talking to? We may adjust our styles so that others will better understand and respond to us. We do this at a subconscious level. How much better and easier might this process be if we could use a simple, proactive and conscious method to make the proper adjustments needed to communicate more effectively?

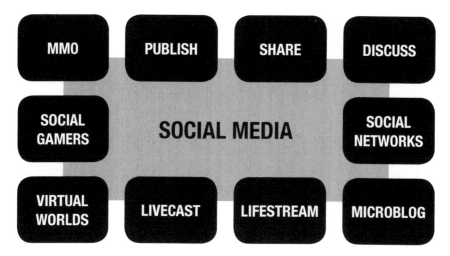

However, remember that talking face-to-face is only one of many communications options. In person, we can consider body language, tone of voice, facial expressions and more. Unfortunately, such face-to-face communications are on the decline and make our communications efforts even more difficult.

You see, we live in a new world of communications. We will cover this later, but, the new model of social media communications is one that we must consider.

So, personal and face-to-face communications seem a lot easier when we consider our noisy world. And, remember the simple model from before. Our world is not so basic anymore—it is global and never stops.

So, not only do we have to deal with written communications, we have to deal with them in a myriad of formats. With the advent of social media, we text, Skype, email, tweet, blog, facebook and more. The list goes on (you get the idea) and surely will expand into even newer methods. Communications are more important than ever. Nobody can be an expert at every type of communications; however, the secret is to pick the tools that work best for you and your audience and become great at using them.

To compete and be successful in all aspects of life, you must become a skilled communicator. There is more noise than ever to compete with to successfully get your message to and understood by the receiver.

So, can we apply the *Everyone is in Sales* philosophy to all forms of communications?

Yes, we can. The process is *Adaptive Communications*. The next chapter will introduce this powerful concept.

SECTION II

The Adaptive Communications Model

CHAPTER 5

Adaptive Communications Overview

So, what is *adaptive communications* and why does it matter? What will it do for you? What does this mean? How will it help you sell your ideas and motivate others? Good question…and I'm glad you were thinking in such a manner.

Adaptive communications is the cornerstone of the *Everyone Is in Sales* philosophy. It is a powerful way of understanding how we can maximize our interactions with others so we can effectively communicate with them. It impacts every aspect of our lives.

In business, it can help us conduct more effective meetings. In social media, it can help ensure that we understand how what we are writing might be perceived. At the baseball field, it can make us better coaches. In addition, it can help each of us become a better spouse, parent, sibling and friend.

If you are looking for a job, it will give you an edge. At your child's school, it will help you find common ground with your child's teacher. It can help you approach all of your personal and professional interactions more effectively. Simply stated, by following these principles, you will reduce stress, conflict and misunderstandings.

And remember, as mentioned before, *misunderstandings= miscommunications* in every part of life. The advantages of understanding adaptive communications are countless, and none of us can afford to overlook these tools.

Does this mean we will always communicate in an effective manner? Of course not—we are human beings. This is not some gimmick or silver-bullet communications strategy I am sharing. To the contrary, it is based on time-tested truths and rooted in my rigorous academic training. The good news is that I have made this simple to understand so it can be remembered, used effectively, and referred to repeatedly. Will your overall success rate of effective communications increase? Yes, more than you will ever believe.

Successful communications are vital in every part of life. They enable us to discover common ground with different individuals, they make the communications process clear and rewarding, and they enable us to better understand ourselves as well as those around us.

There are four areas of adaptive communications that we will cover in detail:

First, is the **speak-first, think-later** group vs. **think-first, speak-later** group. This distinction deals with how a person prefers to direct their energy and expressions (external or internal).

The second component is the **big-picture** vs. the **just-the-facts** group. This segment addresses how people prefer to take in information from the world around them.

The third segment is the **head** vs. **heart** group. This aspect addresses how people make decisions on the information they have taken in.

The final component is the **5 o'clock-sharp** vs. the **5 o'clock-somewhere** group. This component deals with a person's time orientation. For example, do they like to make a decision and have a matter decided or leave things open-ended?

As we begin, let me emphasize that all of us go back and forth between each segment in all four groups. How we respond depends on both the situation and context. Human beings are incredibly complicated, and nobody can simply be labeled as a "this" or "that."

However, we all have definite communications preferences. This means we all have ways and methods within each of the segments regarding how we are most comfortable: talking, taking in information, making decisions on information, or planning things.

For example, if we are a right-handed person, we will likely use our right hand to sign our name, shake hands, throw a ball, and open a jar. Why? Because, it is easier to do with our right hand. It is more comfortable. It is what we are used to doing, and thus we do it without even thinking about it.

Does this mean we are incapable of using our left hand to do these things? Of course not. We can definitely use our left hand; however, if we are right-handed, then we are likely more comfortable with this hand, and thus choose it unconsciously. Thus, this is our "default" or preferred way to do things.

Likewise, we all have a preferred way to communicate with others in the world. Can we communicate differently? Sure we can. But, it is more difficult and does not come as easily (like signing our name with our less preferred hand.) For example, think about signing your name. Can you sign your name with your less preferred hand? Yes. Is this other hand well developed and as comfortable for most of us? No. So, while it can be done, the other side is not as developed as we begin. But can our other less preferred hand improve? Yes. Can we become more comfortable with it? Yes. Is it likely ever going to be as good as our preferred hand? No, and the same is true in our communications.

41

We will naturally communicate more effectively with a person who shares the same style as ours; however, we can become a much better communicator when we learn to "adapt" our preferred communications style to match the situation/context we are in. There are no gimmicks in this process. It is just the opposite.

We learn to appreciate another person's preferred ways of communicating so we can provide them with a message and through a medium that is more apt to be interpreted successfully by them (as the receiver of the message). As we learned in the last chapter, this is what is necessary for successful two-way communications to occur.

> **When "adapting" of communications occurs, we are likely to witness special communications taking place.**

So, in the process of learning adaptive communications, we must first learn and understand our own preferred/default communications style and then learn to recognize the style of others we communicate with. We can and should adjust our style to that of the other person. When "adapting" of communications occurs, we are likely to witness special communications taking place.

The following personal stories are intended to demonstrate how each of the four areas of adaptive communications affects all of our interactions. These stories provide a snapshot of each of the four segments of adaptive communications that will each be discussed in subsequent chapters. By sharing glimpses into communications I have observed between associates, colleagues, and friends, I hope you will begin to see yourself and others in a new way.

Example one: *Speak-First, Think-Later* Group vs. *Think-First, Speak-Later* Group

A few years ago, I observed a conversation between two of my business colleagues, John and Jeff, and the following situation played out. John's preferred method of communications is *speak-first, think-later*. So, picture this. Jeff, who is a *think-first, speak-later* person, comes into John's office for a brief and routine meeting. Jeff sits down for what he expects to be a five minute meeting. Instead, John begins to enthusiastically share (off subject) a series of new ideas, one right after the other.

John throws out idea after idea to Jeff with tremendous enthusiasm and passion. Now keep in mind, most of these concepts were halfway developed at this point in time (although some were good) and were expressed in "brainstorming" mode. I recall John sharing his energy, ideas, and excitement with our colleague in an "unfiltered manner" or what many would call "thinking out loud."

He shared thoughts about new expansions, ventures and opportunities. Jeff simply looked as if he was in a frozen or lost state. Was he totally disinterested? Or, perhaps he just thought John was crazy. Or could it be he simply had no clue what John was talking about?

As John talked, my reflective partner, Jeff, said very little. He simply nodded and listened. I remember that John walked away from that conversation feeling quite deflated. You see, John had expended a lot of external energy in sharing all of his new thoughts with Jeff but had received very little feedback. At least that is how it seemed from John's vantage point.

Now let's look at how this situation was perceived from the other side. Jeff, being one who prefers to think things through before commenting, (*think-first, speak-later*) was simply overwhelmed by this conversation. In fact, it was not really a conversation. It was actually a "one-way monologue" with John talking "at" Jeff.

My partner felt overwhelmed by John's information and was unable to immediately process all of the concepts. He had a hard time following the bombardment of ideas John had thrown at him. My colleague, Jeff, was simply at a loss for words, and thus all he could do was just stare, nod and absorb.

What is interesting—I learned later—was that Jeff really had no opinion (good or bad) about what John was saying at that point. He was simply trying to keep up with John's rapid stream of ideas. He did not think it possible to comment in real time to all John was sharing in his excited state—so he simply absorbed the information.

What happened here is important for us to consider. It appears from what I have said that one colleague, John, was rambling, and my other associate, Jeff, was distant. As it turned out, Jeff was quite excited about several of the possibilities that John had presented. Again, due to Jeff's natural communications style, he needed time to process everything that John had said.

Can you begin to see that the new ideas John was trying to share with Jeff were neither embraced nor discarded by him? Jeff was simply trying to absorb and reflect on all that John was saying. He was visibly quiet and reserved, so John "read" this to mean he was not interested. In turn, John walked away, being a person of high energy and enthusiasm, feeling he had failed and thus presented a bunch of meaningless ideas.

Jeff did not say much about anything to John for a couple of days. This discouraged John all the more as he sought feedback (of any kind). Then, unexpectedly, three days after they had talked, Jeff came into John's office and sat down. Jeff said, "John, you had some great ideas the other day. I needed to reflect on all of these concepts for a few days, but, man, you are on the mark. We need to discuss a couple of these in more detail." John was certainly not expecting this. It was now his turn to be bewildered.

Can you visualize this? John thought his colleague was not interested, but as it turns out, this was not the case. Instead, as Jeff's style is *think-first, speak-later*, he needed time to reflect on all that John had shared with him. However, since John's style was *speak-first, think-later*, he had expected—even if some of his ideas were off base—some immediate feedback. What we have here is two different styles of communications at work. Neither style is right or wrong; and, we all use both of them depending on the context.

This story is a perfect example of the process of ineffective communications at work that we all experience on a regular basis. Two individuals take part in the same conversation, and yet approach it, remember it, and experience it in completely different ways. This is all perception versus reality. John was wrong about what Jeff had thought. Jeff was interested but simply overwhelmed by John's rapid and intense expression of ideas.

It was at this point I met with them and shared the adaptive communications model. They both quickly embraced it. Through the process of adaptive communications, John learned to communicate messages to Jeff—in future settings—in a different way. First, he would tell Jeff in advance that he had a bunch of "raw" ideas to share. In addition, John would tell Jeff that they may or may not be good ideas, but he needed Jeff to help flesh them out and give him some initial feedback (notice the importance of feedback for a *speak-first, think-later* person).

Moreover, the two of them began setting times for their meetings, and both knew in advance what they would be discussing so that neither was caught off guard. Also, John told Jeff it was fine to take a few days to ponder his ideas before responding. Finally, John gave Jeff permission to interrupt him (when he was talking) for clarification, or ask him to slow down if what John was saying was confusing in nature.

This is adaptive communications at work. Both of my colleagues were able to communicate in a new way. A better way. A more effective way. Over time, this became a successful formula for them—all due to the adaptive communications model—that helped both of them improve their interpersonal communications.

The whole point of communications is to sell our ideas to another person. This is most successful when both parties have their communications needs met. When we use one style and throw all of our ideas against the wall to see what sticks, and the person we are speaking to prefers to be given one idea at a time, no ideas are being "sold or bought"—ineffective communications are taking place.

The success of an exchange between a *speak-first, think-later* communicator and a *think-first, speak-later* communicator is minimal at best and an outright failure at its worst. This is why recognizing another's communications style and developing the ability to adapt to this style are so critical.

Example Two: *Big-Picture* vs. *Just-the-Facts* Groups

The next aspect of communications style is the *big-picture* vs. *just-the-facts* types. About a year ago, a friend of mine, Robert, was training a new marketing person in Dallas. The trainee's preferred communications style was *just-the-facts*, whereas Robert's preferred style was *big-picture* in nature. These two styles are based on how a person takes in information about the world.

After they had been working for a couple of hours, Robert told Mark, the marketing trainee, a story in his *big-picture* style. He began by saying how he hoped to win the consulting contract with their San Diego division. Robert went on to say that San Diego was such a beautiful city…and it was only a couple hours drive to Los Angeles…In fact, he'd love to go to LA while out that way…and as Mark was now in the media related business, his goal should be to make it to LA too…It made sense as it was an ideal place for Mark to learn new things about the business…

Robert then went on to share that he had not visited LA in some time…and, it was a short flight from LA to beautiful Hawaii…where he had a speech coming up and was going to take his wife with him…and celebrate their anniversary there, as they had many years before…Robert went on to say he would love to retire in Hawaii…and told Mark that he should really visit Hawaii one day. So, in short order, Robert went from hoping to get a consulting assignment with their San Diego division to talking about retiring in Hawaii.

Well, as you can imagine, there was a problem with this string of "communications." Robert made a lot of statements that, in his stream of consciousness, flowed naturally from one to the next. To the people who are fact/ logic focused, however, his statements do not make much sense.

For example, Mark who preferred *just-the-facts* information was given *big-picture* information that (from his vantage point) illogically jumped from one statement to another. When Robert finished with this story, Mark was looking at him—which Robert told me he will never forget. He said, "Robert, that was a passionate story and sounds awesome, but you lost me at the point where you said you were hoping to do more consulting for us in San Diego. I am not sure I follow all of the other steps that came after, and I am kind of lost."

Robert told me that he felt he had blown it. Here he was a trainer, and the trainee had not been able to follow him. I quickly realized, as Robert told me this story, that he had not adapted his own *big-picture* style of communications to meet Mark's *just-the-facts* style. Thus, he was ineffective in his communications. Not only did Mark lose track of the overall story Robert was trying to share, Mark got lost trying to figure out how Robert had gotten from point number 1 to point 10…as he leapt from one thought to another without connecting the dots for Mark.

So what should Robert have done to improve his communications? We discussed this. First, he should have adapted his *big-picture* communications style to meet the needs of this *just-the-facts* trainee. He should have said: "Do you want to hear a story?" Then he should have asked if Mark had ever been to the San Diego division or San Diego in general.

Robert should have inquired whether Mark had a desire to go and why. Then he should have asked if Mark knew how far LA was from San Diego. Robert should have followed that by asking Mark if he had been to LA, if he wanted to go to LA and if he thought he could learn more about the media business by visiting LA.

He should have then had some fun and asked a trivia question such as: how far is LA from Hawaii? Once Mark answered it, he should have expressed that Mark should go out to Hawaii some time, and shared (on a personal note) this his wife was coming with him to celebrate their anniversary as they did many years ago. Finally, he should have said, "You know, it would be great to retire in Hawaii one day—I love that place!"

This story would have given the marketing trainee, Mark, both a mental break from the arduous training and also met his preferred communications needs for specific, logical, and sequential details of how Robert's story was connected. The communications would have been much more successful if Robert had adapted his communications style to meet Mark's style.

The name of the game is *adaptive communications*. He could have ultimately conveyed the same message by using his "less preferred, left-handed style" of communications (factual and sequential) to match Mark's left-handed and preferred style of communications. Then Mark could have easily followed his message and clearly understood what Robert was trying to communicate.

Example 3: *Head* vs. *Heart* Groups

Another aspect of human communications focuses on how people prefer to make decisions. This is what they do with information once they have absorbed it and what criteria they use to make their decisions.

There are two groups in this third component of the adaptive communications model. The first is known as the *head* group, and the second is called the *heart* group. The *head* group makes more objective decisions and is able to put their emotions aside when making a decision. In contrast, the *heart* group is apt to make more subjective decisions. These individuals tend to interject themselves and their emotions into the decision.

Here is a story that will help us better understand this segment of adaptive communications. This story comes from a company that I helped, in time, explain the adaptive communications model to.

A few years ago, this organization had an employee, Sandy, who had worked in the same division for many years. Andrew was Sandy's manager. Andrew was very loyal to her and Sandy was very dedicated to Andrew. Over the years, Sandy had done a great job for both Andrew and the overall organization. However, things change.

Over time, her life changed, creating issues at work. Her spouse had new job demands, and there were some problems with her kids and more. As a result, Sandy's work performance began to suffer. She began to arrive to work late, and although she was trying hard to make things work, the bottom line was that the company was no longer receiving the high level of performance that her position demanded.

Sandy had a key corporate position, and was paid a good salary to do her job. Quite frankly, she was overpaid for the job, but again this was because of Andrew's loyalty to her and his desire to reward her for a job well done over the years.

You see, Andrew was a part of the *heart* group. He preferred to make more subjective decisions based on the way he felt about a situation (thus with his heart), not necessarily on the hard facts and data (or with his head).

Everyone around Andrew was asking why he kept giving Sandy second chances or "mulligans" to do things over. What made these questions even harder for him to answer was the fact that everyone knew he could hire a better person from the outside and pay them less to do more. So, from a logical point of view, Andrew's thought process made no sense. So why did he keep providing this employee additional chances? It stemmed from his great loyalty to Sandy and his natural style of communications.

It was obvious when Andrew looked at the facts that this person's job performance had indeed declined. Maybe he did not want to see that. Other company leaders, many who were in the *head* group, could not understand Andrew's reluctance to make the required change. What they did not understand—which I quickly saw—was that Andrew's heart was getting in the way of the head-oriented decision that had to be made.

Ultimately, using adaptive communications, I shared with Andrew how to look at this situation in a different way. He began to understand and learned to view these circumstances from a *head* perspective and logical vantage point (his left-handed and less preferred style). Thus, Andrew was able to separate his emotions from the equation and look at this situation in a "black-and-white" manner.

He realized the organization was paying too much, and getting too little in return. He had given too many warnings, and frankly, his own credibility as a leader was at stake. So, he adapted his style and made the only logical decision possible. He let the employee go. Was

50

this easy for him? No. Did he enjoy it? No. Did Andrew's use of adaptive communications change his overall preferred style? No. However, it did allow him to make the necessary and appropriate decision.

This is what adaptive communications is all about. It is about assessing the situation and using either your preferred or non-preferred communications style (whatever will be most effective) to handle a situation. In the early months of Sandy's diminished performance, it made sense to cut her some slack. After all, bad things happen to all of us at times, and Andrew had been supportive.

However, when things did not get better over a longer period of time, and Sandy did not improve her performance after repeated warnings, providing more time was no longer a smart plan. Andrew had only one option. It was time to adapt from the *heart* group to the *head* group.

Even though it was uncomfortable and somewhat unnatural for him to base his decision solely on the hard data/facts rather than the feelings/appreciation for all Sandy had done to help him and the organization over the years, this was necessary. Adapting our communications to match a particular person, situation or context is a critical component of the *Everyone Is in Sales* mindset.

In this last segment, we will look at two groups who have a difference in time orientation as it relates to the world around them. We have the *5 o'clock-sharp* group and the *5 o'clock-somewhere* group. As you can probably ascertain from the two names, the two groups deal with differences in a person's desired time orientation and scheduling.

Example 4: *5 o'clock-Sharp* Group vs. *5 o'clock-Somewhere* Group

We all do both of these things, but one is more comfortable to us. Here is a recent story that occurred while I was on vacation.

I was on a week's vacation with my family and some friends in Florida. What I observed between two people, soon after arriving, was a classic battle between the *5 o'clock-sharp* group and the *5 o'clock-somewhere* group. The *5 o'clock-somewhere* friend, Craig, saw this as a week he could "go with the flow." In his mind, time and hard dates were suspended for the week…or so he thought.

One of my other friends, Veronica, who is part of the *5 o'clock-sharp* group, quickly challenged his deadline-free vacation plans. Craig and I had planned to play golf once during the week that we were there. It was fine with everyone for us to play golf, so we assumed there was no problem as to which day we played. We were wrong.

What became problematic was (and we can apply this scenario to a myriad of places in our lives) which day we were going to play golf. You see, we had arrived on a Saturday and were staying for a week. So from Craig's *5 o'clock-somewhere* mindset, he figured we had plenty of options to consider regarding what day we would play golf. There were at least four viable days that we could choose from. Remember, we were on vacation—one of the few times in a 12-month period where everyone did not have to plan every aspect of life.

Veronica did not embrace Craig's plan (to keep our golf date open-ended). Why? Because it did not meet her communications need of promptly scheduling a precise time slot for golf. She really wanted a decision from us after we arrived as to what day we were going to play golf. Craig asked her why it mattered.

She said, "We need to get it on the calendar, have it decided, so we can plan and enjoy the rest of the week." Craig said again, "I don't know what day I want to play or what time I want to play— we just got here…who cares? We are on vacation." Well, this did not work so well either.

She said, "If you want to make everyone happy, please call, pick a day and time, and make your tee-time so we can get some closure on this and make our other plans. Then, we can begin having some fun." As you can see this was really important to her. I saw what was going on and called a "guys timeout." I explained to Craig what adaptive communications was, what was going on here, and gave him some advice on how to adapt his style. After doing this, Craig, had a better understanding of where Veronica was coming from and adapted his communications style to accommodate her communications needs. His style of keeping things open-ended was frustrating to her and did not meet what she was looking for in a vacation.

Always, remember there is no right or wrong... just two different ways of looking at something. For a *5 o'clock-sharp* person to have fun and relax, they need to have all the details and variables worked out/planned in advance. They do not like matters left open-ended, nor do they like last-minute surprises.

So, since she is a friend—and it was important to maintain harmony—Craig met her *5 o'clock-sharp* communications needs (and I helped him as I figured this would be a good book story at some point...and it is). Reluctantly, Craig made a firm decision about the day and time we would play golf, even though it was still not his preference to do so.

Craig used his new found knowledge of adaptive communications to adjust his preferred style to better communicate with Veronica and meet her *5 o'clock-sharp* needs. This way she could relax and enjoy her vacation. He adapted his natural right-handed style of *5 o'clock-somewhere* to his less preferred left-handed *5 o'clock-sharp* communications style to meet the needs of the situation. And guess what? Adaptive communications saved the day. Everyone was happy—including me as I just wanted to play golf. I enjoyed knowing which day I would spend all day searching for golf balls... oops...I meant playing golf.

All four of the segments above are real stories (with some name changes for the sake of privacy) that help us remember and recall the four components of the adaptive communications model. We will be going through each of the four segments in great detail in the upcoming chapters but this this chapter serves as an overview. I always say that theory is great, however, without real world and practical application (which we can see through these stories) a theory is hard to follow and embrace.

So, now you have seen some different styles in action. The more quickly you embrace adaptive communications—a subject I do lots of training sessions on—the faster you will learn to use both your *left-handed and right-handed styles*—as need be to meet your communications objectives.

Have you thought about default communications styles? If not, you will be able to soon enough. So, buckle your seatbelts, again, folks, as we are about to embark on a more in-depth journey into adaptive communications. And, remember adaptive communications is one of the fundamental cornerstones of the *Everyone Is in Sales* philosophy

CHAPTER 6

Speak-First, Think-Later vs. Think-First, Speak-Later Group

When I shared the story about Jeff and John's communications exchange, I did it to illustrate a real world situation. In this instance, we showed how a *speak-first, think-later* person can fail to communicate with a *think-first, speak-later* person. My business partners were saying words, in the same room, but were not communicating in an effective manner.

So, in this chapter, my desire is to share some of the characteristics you will see in each group. My goal is for you to be able to readily identify your preferred communications style as well as that of the other person you are communicating with. Remember, it is always going to be easier to communicate with and sell your position to someone in the same group you are in.

At the end of the chapter, you will find a list of questions that will help you be certain as to your preferred style. We will review simple ways to overcome communications obstacles and differences so that we can reach a point of compatibility between the two different communications styles, because this is where a lot of *misunderstandings = miscommunications* occur.

There are some general characteristics that each of these two types tend to display. This makes identifying which type you prefer and what type the other person likes very important in the adaptive communications process. So let's take a look at some ways to understand and contrast the people who would be in the *speak-first, think-later* group with those who would be in the *think-first, speak-later* group.

Most *speak-first, think-later* types appear self-confident. They are social and love lots of interaction with others. They love to discuss a breadth of topics and move from one to another. They usually have a relaxed and approachable nature and are personable. *Speak-first, think-later* persons are apt to "let it all out," however, after doing so; they generally get mad at themselves for not keeping their mouth shut.

Because they have confidence in themselves, it is easy for this group to share what's on their mind. You see, they view their ideas as being of value to others. The concepts in their minds are "talked out loud," meaning they may not be well developed, but this is how they think through their ideas. They are sociable and expressive. You are likely to see this type in sales, politics or public relations to name a few.

Think of the most outgoing person you know. Think about them in a myriad of settings you have seen them in. Do they tend to have some or all of these characteristics? Maybe you are thinking of a friend that loves to be the life of the party. He or she may be the former class president or head cheerleader. Do they tend to have lots of "friends?" Do they seem to have a hard time listening?

Perhaps you think of someone who dabbles in local politics or is the top local realtor. These people love to try new things, promote new ideas and quickly take initiative in all relationships. They may start a conversation by saying, "Hey listen, I have a great idea, let's…"

In contrast, people in the *think-first, speak-later* group appear reserved and quiet. This type of person is disposed to having a set of closely held values. They work through issues internally before sharing their thoughts with others. This means they think things out "inside their head" not out loud. You hear persons in this group say, "Let me think about it."

They appear shy, private or contained. They tend to focus their attention in depth on a few things. They are good listeners. They prefer written over verbal communications. Reflecting on an idea is more important to them than taking immediate action. When they communicate, it is marked by subtlety and understatement. Engineers, accountants, librarians, researchers and IT professionals tend to fall in this group.

> *Once you know your style, it becomes your responsibility to adapt to those you are communicating with (whether as the sender or receiver of a message).*

For example, picture your high school science teacher. He likely focused his attention on fewer things, used words sparingly and was not overly expressive. Moreover, this person—and I can picture one—loved to reflect on deep matters and liked to take his time to do so. However, when he did make a statement it was almost always well thought out and intelligent in nature.

But guess what? Although it is important to understand and recognize another person's type, this is of secondary importance to fully comprehending your own communications style. Once you know your style, it becomes your responsibility to adapt to those you are communicating with (whether as the sender or receiver of a message).

This is how you will be more successful in your communications and embrace the *Everyone Is in Sales* mentality. Let's look at some questions so you can identify your own preference.

1. Would you prefer to go to a party with lots of people or stay home and have one close friend come over? (go to party = *speak-first*, stay home = *think-first*)

2. When you get a new idea, do you call a few people and run it by them or make some notes and take some time to reflect and think it through? (call a few people = *speak-first*, will make notes/reflect = *think-first*)

3. In a new setting, are you more likely to introduce yourself to a stranger and strike up a conversation, or do you tend to wait for others to come to you and introduce themselves? (introduces themselves to others = *speak-first*, wait for people to introduce themselves to you = *think-first*)

4. When you watch a political candidate speak, do you spend time reflecting on what the candidate said, or are you more likely to jump to a quick conclusion regarding what he said? (jump to conclusions = *speak-first*, reflecting = *think-first*)

5. Which style do you admire more; that of Albert Einstein or General Patton? (admire Patton = *speak-first*, admire Einstein = *think-first*)

6. Do you like to work at a rapid pace and move from one task to another, or do you like to work at a slower pace and in a more methodical/ in-depth manner? (rapid pace = *speak-first*, methodical = *think-first*)

7. Do you like to wear more expressive/colorful attire that draws attention to you, or do you prefer to wear clothing

that is more subdued/reserved and does not call attention to you? (expressive = *speak-first*, reserved = *think-first*)

If you feel more comfortable with the *speak-first* responses, your preferred communications group is *speak-first, think-later*. In contrast, if you find yourself relating to the *think-first* responses, your preferred communications type is *think-first, speak-later.*

OK, so now you know how to identify your own preferred communications style, but how do you identify the style of others? It is critical that you identify—as much as possible—the other person's preferred type of communications.

After all, understanding both sides is a premise of adaptive communications. You must know your own style and another's style well enough that you can adapt your communications as either the sender or receiver so a message can be successfully communicated.

If you do not know the preferences of the person you are communicating with, it will be difficult to know if your message has been received and correctly understood. Here are some questions to ask yourself to determine what the other person's communications style is:

1. Does she look me in the eye when she speaks? (yes = *speak-first*; no = *think-first*)

2. Does he smile and seem relaxed, or does he seem tentative and tense? (relaxed = *speak-first*; tense = *think-first*)

3. Is he quick to open up or slow to open up to you? (quick to open up = *speak-first*; slow to open up = *think-first*)

4. Does she engage in small talk or get right to the subject at hand? (small talk = *speak-first*; right to the subject = *think-first*)

5. When you ask, "How's business?" he answers, "Fine" or, "Man, business is booming." ("booming" = *speak-first*; "fine" = *think-first*)

By evaluating the answers to these questions, you can better understand the preferences of another person and adapt your approach to accommodate their style. Then effective communications will have a much better chance of taking place.

Now let's look at some simple examples to illustrate adaptive communications in action. First, let's consider an easy one. Let's say your preferred communications style is *speak-first, think-later*, and you are trying to communicate with a client who has this same preference in communications. What do you do? Well first, your natural tendencies will likely resonate well with this other person. Simply said, you will feel comfortable communicating with them. In addition, you can use your enthusiasm to transmit these feelings to your client. When you talk, you will be able to let your ideas flow in a natural way.

The client will appreciate your openness and sharing of information. Why? Because you are talking to them in their preferred mode of communications, and thus it is easy for them to follow. So let's look at how this scenario plays out.

You call on Linda, the owner of a local costume store, to promote a new line of vampire costumes…

"Hey, Linda. How's it going?"

Linda says, "Things are crazy busy here. How's your business doing?"

"Well," you say. "Now that we've introduced our new line of vampire attire, things are booming. We are selling them as fast as we can make them. I didn't want you to miss out on this hot trend and money that can be made with them."

"Thanks," Linda says. "Show me what you have, and if it can help us keep growing, I am on board."

When you and your client have the same communications style, communications naturally go well, because you both "speak the same language." But lets now use another example. What if you *speak-first* are now trying to communicate with a co-worker who is in the *think-first* group?

The first thing you must do is slow down and develop a plan. You must recognize that your co-worker is unlikely to respond well to your natural *speak-first, think-later* type. Instead, you should consider the topic to be covered, what you want the outcome to be, and how best to adapt your style to match that of your co-worker's preference.

Picture the following adaptive exchange between you and Jim, the project manager. You need his division to "ramp up" the rollout because of heavy demand for the new product. Your natural tendency would be to grab him in the hall, tell him how great sales are going, shoot from the hip and quickly tell him you need him to get the new product rolling ASAP. At best, Jim would have little idea of what you were talking about. Instead this approach would be more effective:

"Hey, Jim. I need to talk with you about the product rollout that begins next month. I have some questions about the time line and other specific logistical questions because our presales have been more successful than expected. Could you meet in my office at 2 p.m. today?"

Jim responds, "What information do you want me to bring? I have all of the project flow charts if you would like to see them."

"Thanks, Jim, but all I need to see is the number of units that will be available and the rollout schedule,

so we can estimate a realistic delivery date to the customers."

As you adapted your communications style to meet Jim's needs everything went quite well. Jim's preferred communications style and needs have been met, and he has been given the necessary information about what you need and why you need it.

In addition, you provided him time to consider how to answer your questions and reflect on ways to help you achieve your goals. So, through the use of adaptive communications you accomplished your goals by meeting Jim's communications needs. You did this through developing a careful plan, being specific, providing him pre-warning of the meeting, and giving him time to prepare.

What if we look at it a different way? What if you happen to be part of the *think-first* group and you are talking to someone who is also in the *think-first* group? Once again the communications process is comfortable and apt to be successful as you are talking the "same language." Imagine that you are calling your dad, who is part of the same communications group as you, to find out how his visit to the doctor went yesterday. The conversation is likely to go something like this:

"Hello, Dad. I just wanted to make sure everything's OK."

"Thanks, Son. Things aren't too bad."

"Well, did the doctor give you any idea what is making you feel so dizzy?"

"Not yet. He wants to run some tests first before he makes any diagnosis...Depending on what he finds we will create an appropriate treatment plan. Things should be fine."

"OK, Dad, sounds like you have things under control. Keep me posted."

With communications styles that are similar, you can quietly ask your dad how he is, and he can quickly share as much as he wants to with you—without unnecessary drama—and you understand. You were thus able to find out how he is and what the doctor said, which was your goal, while making him feel at ease.

If you are a *think-first* type addressing a *speak-first* type, adaptive skill is needed to accomplish your objective. Picture this situation: You, as a *think-first* type, need to have a conversation with your oldest daughter about her curfew. By the way, she is a *speak-first* type.

"Jenna, I need for us to talk after dinner tonight. We need to rationally discuss your curfew. I know how important this issue is to you, so we need to come to an agreement that you will like, while making sure your safety always comes first. OK?"

"Dad, I told you I want to stay out to midnight because all of my friends get to. What's there to talk about?"

"Jenna, I know how you feel, and we will talk as much as we need to tonight about it. Let's just both think about how the curfew impacts everyone. OK?"

After dinner, Jenna begins, "Dad, please let me stay out with my friends until midnight. I really don't want to be embarrassed by having to come home at 11:00 like a baby."

"Jenna, you are not a baby, and I don't want to treat you like one. I mean it. Unfortunately there are other very important issues involved here. You know that there have been random attacks in the late evening

by gangs. I know you would never put yourself near those gangs on purpose, but they are showing up all over town. Your Mom and I would be devastated if something happened to you or any of your friends."

"I know, Dad, but I am really careful."

"I wish it were something you could control by being careful, but it isn't. Let me propose a solution that will help keep you safe, while giving you more freedom. How about we make a deal that when you are with friends hanging out, that you come home at 11:00? Blame it on your overly cautious parents. When you are going to a specific place for the whole evening, we will set midnight as your curfew."

"Dad, if I am really careful can we make it 11:30 when I'm hanging out, please?"

"Jenna, I understand how you feel, but I trust you to understand how Mom and I feel, too. Please let's agree to try the plan I suggested for a month. Then we can re-evaluate how things are going. OK, honey?"

"OK, but we really will talk again in a month, right?"

"We sure will. And thanks for being willing to make Mom and I feel better about your safety."

By adjusting your *think-first* style that prefers quiet discussion about the value of an earlier or later curfew, to accommodate Jenna's animated *speak-first* style, you had a successful string of communications where both sides listened.

You explained that you understood her position and quickly pointed out that she was not a baby, but there were other things (such as danger) to consider. By doing this, you enabled her to see beyond her own impulsive desires, and gave her a lot more to consider.

Further, by getting her to wait to discuss the issue later, rather than get into an argument in the hallway, when you brought the subject up; you addressed the situation in a timely, but not immediate, manner. You allowed her some time—wanted or not— to reflect on the issue, taking into account your concerns.

Adaptive communications is powerful and improves the quality and results of interactions, whether it is between co-workers, clients, friends or family members. And (here is the best part) this is only 25 percent of the puzzle that I have presented so far. I told you this would be a book you would refer to many times. Below you will find some strategies to consider when thinking about the groups of *speak-first, think-later* and *think-first, speak-later*. Strategies for adapting between *speak-first* and *think-first* types include:

If you are a *speak-first, think-later* person communicating to a *think-first, speak-later* person:

- Slow down and plan what you are going to say.

- Calm down and operate at a slower pace.

- Decide what you want to accomplish before you ever begin the conversation.

- Speak in specific terms/concepts when possible.

- Do not overwhelm them with too much information at one time.

- Acknowledge the need for the other person to reflect on what you are proposing.

- Be willing to allow the other person additional time to review your ideas.

- Do not finish their sentences/statements for them.

- Communicate in written form when you can.

- Discuss one subject fully before moving to another.

If you are *a think-first, speak-later* person communicating to a *speak-first, think-later* person:

- Put more energy and enthusiasm than normal into your discussion.

- Display full confidence in what you are saying.

- Share many ideas of what can be accomplished.

- Be expressive and move at a quicker pace when making your points.

- Be ready to think on your feet and operate at a faster speed than normal.

- Have as much information as possible available "at your fingertips" to share.

- Acknowledge the other's potential need to get started right away.

- Communicate in a verbal fashion (in person) if possible.

- Be prepared to quickly move from one topic to another.

- Include a variety of subjects/topics in your conversation.

In the next three chapters, we will use this format to examine the other three other groups in adaptive communications. Included will be descriptions of the styles, questions to identify styles and types, and recommendations for adapting communications. The fun is just beginning.

CHAPTER 7

Big-Picture Group vs. Just-the-Facts Group

The second component of adaptive communications focuses on how people "take in" information from the world around them. This has nothing to do with the decision they ultimately make on the information, but is simply about how they prefer to receive the information. Remember the story I shared in Chapter 5 about Robert, the consultant, talking about San Diego with the marketing trainee? It provides a great segway into this chapter.

Big-picture persons have great vision and are quite intuitive in their thinking.

In learning the adaptive communications model, you must consider both your preferences and that of others in regard to how each person takes in information. For example, do you and the person you are communicating with take in information in the same manner or in two different ways?

Again, as we did in the last chapter, we should first consider who we are communicating with. For instance, when we are communicating with someone who prefers taking in information in the same way we do, communications are more comfortable and thus, what I call *right-handed to right-handed* in nature.

In contrast, when we are communicating with someone who takes in information differently than we do, this is what I call *right-handed to left-handed communications*. Thus, one person would need to adapt their style to meet the communications needs of the other person.

In this chapter, we look at the second type of differences in human beings. This is based on how a person takes in information. The first person is part of the *big-picture* group, and prefers to take in the world with a "what could be/gut feel" attitude. The second person is part of the *just-the-facts* group and seeks "concrete/ sequential" details when taking in information.

Big-picture persons want an overview of information, and do not want to hear all the details. *Big-picture* types focus on possibilities and are future-focused in taking in the world around them. They may argue that $3 \times 3 = 9$ is not something to memorize but instead an example of multiplication. They are quick to "connect dots" and anticipate things before they occur.

Big-picture persons have great vision and are quite intuitive in their thinking. When presented with a concept, they approach it by anticipating the future and asking, "what if," "what could be" or "what this could lead to...." This group relies on their "sixth sense" or "gut feel" as they take in the world.

Just-the-facts types are quite the opposite. *Just-the-facts* persons want logical and step-by-step details. They do not want the quick overview as mentioned above since this does not meet their communications needs. They prefer to receive the facts: who, what, where, when, why and how. In addition, they like information that is logical, sequential, and easy to follow.

They do not like having to "connect dots" to determine what something means. They use words such as "this means" or "what we have here" or "the facts suggest…" They are oriented to and live in the present, focusing on what *is* rather than what *could be*.

The *just-the-facts* group would argue that *3 x 3 = 9* is a multiplication fact to memorize rather than an example of multiplication. This group trusts information that they have learned from past experiences. Moreover, they rely on tradition and history as a predictor of what will occur in the future. This influences the way this group takes in information.

As stated before, we all move back and forth between these two groups. However, we all have a definite and default preference in regard to how we take in information. Let's look at the type of information you prefer. In order to help determine this, I have listed some questions for you to consider.

1. Is a rose a textured flower with sharp thorns, or is it the representation of beauty and love? (representation of love = *big picture,* sharp thorns = *just-the-facts*)

2. Given a choice, do you prefer reading a factual how-to book or reading a book that discusses new ideas? (new idea book = *big-picture,* how-to book = *just-the-facts*)

3. In a conversation, do you want to be given specific examples or be provided with a variety of possibilities? (possibilities = *big-picture,* specific examples = *just-the-facts*)

4. When presented with a new concept, do you reflect on how something similar has worked in the past, or do you imagine how this could affect the future? (affect the future = *big-picture,* reflect on past = *just-the-facts*)

5. Does the concept of making a big decision based on a gut feeling make sense or sound foolish to you? (makes sense = *big-picture,* foolish = *just-the-facts*)

6. Do you prefer to have someone teach you in a sequential/
   step-by-step manner or give you the overview and let you
   figure out how things connect? (you figure it out = *big-
   picture*, sequential manner = *just-the-facts*)

7. Which phrase most appeals to you: "This is how we have
   always done it," or "This is a new way we could look at
   doing it?" (new way = *big-picture*, have always done it =
   just-the-facts)

It is essential as we learn adaptive communications not only to
understand our own styles but also the preferences of those with
whom we communicate. Through such understanding, we can
adapt our communications as needed to be most effective.

Here are some ways to determine what group another person
is part of:

1. Do they speak in concrete terms about the world around
   them, or do they talk about future possibilities? (possibilities
   = *big-picture*, concrete = *just-the-facts*)

2. When giving directions, do they say, "Drive a little bit
   further and bear left near a gas station," or "Go ½ mile and
   take a sharp left before you get to the ABC gas station?"
   (near a gas station = *big-picture*, sharp left = *just-the-facts*)

3. When discussing football, do they describe the running
   back as having a 4.4 speed or that the running back's dad
   and uncle also played football? (dad and uncle = *big-
   picture*, 4.4 speed = *just-the-facts*).

4. When standing on the beach, do they describe what the
   sunset might symbolize or explain how the water feels on
   their feet? (sunset = *big-picture*, water on their feet = *just-
   the-facts*)

5. At a nice restaurant, do they imagine how they could create
   an even better restaurant or do they marvel at the cleanliness

and quality of the restaurant? (even better restaurant = *big-picture,* cleanliness and quality = *just-the-facts*)

These are just a few ways to help you determine whether a person's preference is that of the *big-picture* or *just-the-facts* group. There are many other questions you can ask, but this gives you some tangible questions to think about. The key is to make an assessment and determine the other person's preference so you can best communicate with them.

Here is an example of a *big-picture* person talking to a *just-the-facts* person using the adaptive communications model. Notice the *big-picture* person, Bill, has adapted his style to be logical and sequential in nature to meet the needs of Allen, his partner in the restaurant business, who is a *just-the-facts* person.

> *Bill says, "Allen, there is a lot of growth on the east side of town, but we have not picked up much new business from it. I've laid out a step-by-step plan to go after new business. Can we sit down and go over it?"*
>
> *"Sure", says Allen, "Let me get a note pad and pen first. OK, what are you proposing we do?"*
>
> *"Well, first we need to identify the kind of people who are moving into the neighborhood. The condo residents appear to be quite busy and health conscious. We could capitalize on this by offering full takeout meals and delivery services."*
>
> *"Secondly, we can update our menu to include more vegetarian and low-carb dishes, since the condo folks, as I learned in last week's restaurant association meeting, like these healthy offerings. At the meeting, the other restaurants said these new offerings had increased their profitability. I think this would be the case for us as well. What do you think?"*

"Well", Allen replies, "This is a logical plan; I could change a few of my recipes to be low-carb. Also, I read the newest chef's magazine and just learned how to make some great vegetarian dishes. If it is working for our competitors, we should try it. Let me get back to you next week with some specific recipes. In the meantime, will you research how much it would cost us to set up a delivery service?"

So, based on the example above, Bill conveyed his ideas in a factual, sequential and logical manner so that he could meet the needs of Allen's *just-the-facts* communications preference. Thus, as we can see, successful two-way communications occurred.

Now let's look at this situation from the opposite direction. If you are a *just-the-facts* person, Allen, talking to your partner, Bill, part of the *big-picture* group, you will have to adapt your communications as well. Here is the scenario.

"Hey Bill, I've been thinking about ways to take our restaurant to the next level. Restaurants are booming in this city. If we make changes now, we too can grow in a big way. Who knows, we may be able to expand all over the metro area. So, what do you think? Can you see the future, my friend? Let's start by expanding our menu and offering a delivery service. You know those people living in condos will be ordering from us all the time."

In addition, what do you think about offering more menu options with low-carb and vegetarian dishes that provide a healthy alternative? And just think, we can post this all over social media and offer a discount for first-time customers. This could be really big Bill, just think of all of the extra income."

Those are all goods ideas, Allen. I love it. You are thinking in a new way and looking toward the future—that is what it takes in business. I agree! Let's concentrate on developing the new menu and figure out how to start a delivery service. Great idea."

In this second example, Allen spoke in Bill's preferred *big-picture* language. As we can see, Bill, who loves the future, ideas and possibilities, immediately connected with Allen's thinking. In both of these examples a person adapted his preferred communications style to meet the needs of the other.

They worked hard to speak the other's "language" and to talk *right-handed to right-handed in nature* to make the communications successful. This is *adaptive communications* at work. If you are talking to a person who has the same style as you, it is much easier. In this case, use your natural communications preference and you will not need to adapt your communications significantly.

Strategies for adapting your *big-picture* style to the *just-the-facts* type:

- Outline your overall points in a logical manner before you begin talking.

- Present your information in a factual manner.

- For every statement, present evidence that appeals to the five senses.

- Be clear about your objectives and show examples of how your proposed outcome has worked in the past.

- Limit your use of words and phrases such as "imagine" or "picture this."

- Have examples that back up your statements.

- Be sure to finish each sentence before jumping on to another subject.

- Emphasize the practical application of your ideas.

Strategies for adapting your *just-the-facts* style to the *big-picture* type.

- Layout a picture in your mind of possibilities and future implications.

- Paint a word picture of what could be.

- Make your comments creative and inspirational.

- For each statement, present a vision of where it could lead.

- Use analogies and stories in your statements.

- Avoid discussing details and instead focus on broad themes.

- Brainstorm concepts of possibilities for the future.

- Talk about the "gray" you see rather than the black and white.

Well, we are halfway there. In the next chapter we will explore the third component of adaptive communications. This is the *head* versus the *heart* group.

CHAPTER 8

Head vs. Heart Group

In the previous chapter, we explained the two ways people prefer to take in information. However, we left out a key component regarding information and the decision making process. There is no need to worry—I did this intentionally. In the last chapter, we addressed how a person prefers to absorb information, but I did not explain how they make decisions regarding this information once they have taken it in.

Every piece of data we collect goes into a "decision making filter." This may be a conscious or subconscious process. Our preferred way for making a decision on the information we have taken in is the focus of this chapter. We examine the question of how people make decisions—do they prefer to make a decision with their *head* or prefer to make it with their *heart*? These different styles are at opposite ends of the spectrum. Everyone uses both styles at some point; however, every person has a "natural" decision-making style.

So let's build on what we learned in the last chapter. A *big-picture* person could make a decision on the data that was collected with his *head* or his *heart*. On the other hand, a *just-the-facts* person could make a decision on the information that was taken in with her *head* or her *heart*.

This means that even in this simple way of explaining adaptive communications there are four different styles of decision making:

1. *Big-picture* (take in) and *head* (decide with)

2. *Big-picture* (take in) and *heart* (decide with)

3. *Just-the-facts* (take in) and *head* (decide with)

4. *Just-the-facts* (take in) and *heart* (decide with).

Are you starting to see how complex human beings are and why it is important to learn adaptive communications? I hope so. By the way, you will likely need to read and re-read these chapters for this to become second nature. Don't worry—this is the norm.

As a reminder, the s*peak-first, think-later* versus *think-first, speak-later* groups are identified by a person's tendency to say something out loud before thinking it through in contrast to the latter group that tends to reflect on something before commenting.

The second component we looked at was the *big-picture* versus *just-the-facts* groups. This discussion centered on how people prefer to take in information about the world around them. The *big-picture* group is more apt to trust their sixth sense/gut feeling, whereas the *just-the-facts* group seeks detailed/factual information. So this brings us to this *head* versus *heart* chapter. How does a person go about processing and making decisions with the information they have taken in? Are they more comfortable making a decision with their *head* or their *heart*?

Let's go back to the story I shared about Andrew and Sandy. Remember Andrew, the division manager, and his strong loyalty to Sandy who worked for him? Andrew overlooked the objective/ hard data of Sandy's steadily declining performance, because he was more comfortable relying on subjective criteria and his feelings in evaluating her performance. Andrew's preference was to make a decision with his *heart,* but ultimately he adapted his style and made a decision with his *head* in order to address Sandy's declining performance. So, with that story in mind, let's take a look at both the *head* and *heart* groups and some characteristics of each.

The *head* group is comprised of individuals who make decisions in an objective and logical manner. They rely on factual information to make a decision. The *head* group is focused on the task at hand and not on people's feelings when making a decision. In this group, the end result justifies the means of getting there. The *head* group is comfortable taking a step back, detaching their emotions from a situation, and making an objective decision. To those who are not in this group, such decisions may seem cold, uncaring or tough.

Head people are firm and see rules as just that—rules that are made to be followed. For the *head* group, rules are not open for discussion. Simply said, they are what they are. This group's focus on facts, data and logic tends to make them seem distant or uncaring. The *head* group is painfully honest. They view their surroundings, including people, objectively and see the world as "black and white." The *head* group makes decisions based on a methodical and logical analysis of the situation.

In contrast to the *head* group is the *heart* group. People in the *heart* group place great importance on people. Their *heart* preference makes them more personable, casual and emotional. They have a difficult time separating themselves from the actual problem. Whereas the *head* group, as we noted above, can look at a situation objectively, the *heart* group looks at the issue in a subjective manner. They tend to interject their own feelings and beliefs into the problem and become emotionally involved and attached.

77

Individuals in the *heart* group take criticism personally and are quite sensitive. They are tactful when they speak and consider subjective matters and allow room for "gray" areas to be discussed. They see rules as being important but open for review and optional, depending on the situation. The *heart* group's focus is on how people are treated. The *heart* group relies on their emotions rather than hard data to make decisions. They worry about hurting another person's feelings and work hard to please others. In addition, they want people to like them and seek harmony.

The story of Andrew's (*heart* group) loyalty to Sandy is a situation where a person let his emotions override logic. In this case, he overlooked, for a long while, the hard facts and postponed making the *head* decision that was needed. As we know, he ultimately adapted his style and made the correct and objective decision to terminate Sandy. However, as you could see, this was not easy for him.

Let's look at how you prefer to make a decision. In order to help you, I have listed some questions for you to consider.

1. When an idea is presented, do you reflect on how its implementation might impact others or simply if the idea will work? (idea will work = *head,* impact others = *heart*)

2. Are you more often described as a "warm" person who is easy to get to know or a "cold" person who seems distant? (cold = *head,* warm = *heart*)

3. Do you tend to be assertive or lack assertiveness? (assertive = *head,* lack assertiveness = *heart*)

4. When someone asks you a "dumb/redundant" question do you respond in a tactful way or in a blunt manner? (blunt = *head,* tactful = *heart*)

5. Do you use a person's name frequently or infrequently when talking to them? (infrequently = *head,* frequently = *heart*).

6. Do you seek input from others when making a decision, or do you work alone using the facts you have to make a logical analysis? (logical analysis = *head,* input from others = *heart*)

7. When working on a project, which is more important to you; the relationships you build along the way, or simply completing the task? (completing the task = *head,* relationships you build = *heart*)

It is important as we learn adaptive communications not only to understand our own styles but also the preferences of those we communicate with. Through such awareness, we can adapt our communications as needed to be most effective. Here are some ways to determine what group another person is part of:

1. Does the person come across as being distant or friendly? (distant = *head,* friendly = *heart*)

2. Does the person seek to find arguments/conflict or to avoid arguments/conflict? (seek arguments = *head,* avoid arguments = *heart*)

3. When asked their opinion on a matter, does the person boldly state their opinion or "beat around the bush" to determine what answer will please you? (boldly state = *head,* please you = *heart*)

4. Is the person sensitive or insensitive to what is going on in your life? (insensitive = *head,* sensitive = *heart*)

5. Does the person want everyone in a group treated the same or everyone to be treated in an individual manner? (treated the same = *head,* individual manner = *heart*)

Here is an example of a *heart* person talking to a *head* person using the adaptive communications model. Notice the *heart* person, McKenna, has adapted her emotional style to be analytical in nature to meet the needs of Joan, who is a *head* person.

McKenna and Joan both work in a medical office. McKenna and Joan are in charge of planning the office Christmas party. McKenna would normally get excited and appeal to the emotions of the person she is talking to; however, she knows her normal style will not go over well with Joan. So, she adapts her own communications style to meet Joan's communications needs.

McKenna points out all of the reasons they should have a holiday party with a theme and have it a week earlier than usual. McKenna backs up her ideas with research and cost figures and presents it to Joan via email to give her time to review.

Joan likes receiving this type of information so she can spend time analyzing it in order to make a logical decision. Since she could immediately see the logic and benefit of McKenna's idea, Joan agrees that they should move forward.

So what did McKenna do? First, she allowed Joan to make a decision based on the facts and had research/data that she provided to justify why her idea made sense. She communicated in a *right-handed to right-handed* manner (although her own preferred style was left-handed). She knew what appealed to Joan in making a decision, as a member of the *head* group, and it is of little surprise that Joan quickly agreed to her suggestion.

What if we look at it in reverse?

Joan (head preference) is trying to convince McKenna (heart preference) that a Christmas party should have a theme and be a week earlier. Normally, Joan would bluntly say what needed to be done. However, she knew this would not work well with McKenna. So instead, she told McKenna how many

80

more people could make the party if it was a week earlier. She also told McKenna that a theme would make the party more fun and make employees want to bring their families to the party. She then said, "After all isn't the whole point of this Christmas party to make our people feel important?"

Well, guess what? Joan adapted her communications and succeeded as well. McKenna's concern is about people and their feelings in making a decision. Once she knew that these changes would help she was sold on Joan's idea.

Adaptive communications is real, powerful and incredibly effective in all parts of life.

As you can see, once again, *adaptive communications* is real, powerful and incredibly effective in all parts of life.

Strategies for adapting your *heart* style to a *head* type:

- Before you speak, sort out your facts from your feelings— and work with facts.

- Center your remarks on the actual situation and refrain from referencing subjective criteria.

- Be clear that you will outline the issues in a way that leads them to make an informed, objective decision.

- Do not ask them what they "feel or think" about the situation? Stick to the facts.

- Be organized and logical in your comments.

- Avoid repeating yourself.

Strategies for adapting your *head* style to a *heart* type:

Before you speak, realize the other party will take everything you say personally.

- Praise the other person for all they do and their efforts

- Acknowledge in your comments that there are more subjective ways to look at things, but ask that they hear out the facts while you share your position.

- Avoid saying absolute expressions such as "this is the only answer."

- Focus on how the issues will impact people.

- Ask them how they "feel/think" about the situation?

Well, we are 75 percent there. The next chapter on adaptive communications is the fourth and final component. Let's move on to look at a person's orientation with time and closure on matters. We will do this by discussing the *5 o'clock-sharp* group vs. the *5 o'clock-somewhere* group.

CHAPTER 9

5 o'clock-Sharp Group vs.
5 o'clock-Somewhere Group

OK, we are doing great. We have now reached the final chapter of Section II and the last segment of the Adaptive Communications model. This chapter may be last, but is certainly not least.

The *5 o'clock-sharp* versus *5 o'clock-somewhere* component is very important to understand. In many cases, this segment of adaptive communications is where a great deal of conflict and misunderstanding develops. On the other hand, with proper understanding of adaptive communications people can learn to resolve their differences and see things in a new way.

This component of adaptive communications centers on the way people prefer to live their lives. For example, *5 o'clock-sharp* people enjoy living life in an orderly and planned out manner, whereas *5 o'clock-somewhere* people prefer to live life in a flexible and spontaneous fashion. The *5 o'clock-sharp* group prefers to make a decision and have closure on an issue. In contrast, the *5 o'clock-somewhere* group thrives on keeping things open so they are not "locked into" a decision.

Another difference in these two groups is in their orientation to time. The *5 o'clock-sharp* person prefers to get things finished in advance and check them off the list. In contrast, the *5 o'clock-somewhere* person is more comfortable getting things done at the last minute. Can you picture some of these people in your mind?

As you can see, these two groups are quite distinct, and hence this is where tension and misunderstanding can develop. This gap is even greater in our time-sensitive and rapidly moving world, which we cover in greater detail in Section III of this book. The *5 o'clock-sharp* group likes order, closure, and to get things done in advance. To them, arriving at 4:50 or 4:55 is "on time" and arriving at 5:00 is—well…late.

> **To them, arriving close to 5:00 is the same as being on time.**

In contrast, the *5 o'clock-somewhere* group prefers being flexible, keeping things open-ended, and enjoys working until the last minute on a task. This group, special thanks to Jimmy Buffet, is known as the *5 o'clock-somewhere* group. By the way, this does not mean you can check out on me and head to the beach. OK, back to the book. To this group *arriving at 5:00* means that 5:00 is a *suggested* time of arrival. In other words, they will see you in the *range* of 5:00—likely 5:10, 5:15 or so.

To them, arriving close to 5:00 is the same as being on time. This is not because this person is rude, nor is it because the person does not care. In contrast, such individuals generally don't realize that "15 minutes late" offends some people. Most of these people do not intentionally do this.

We all move back and forth between the two groups at different times, but one of them is our "default" group. Think of it this way…if you could orient your day, month, year and/or life in the "perfect" manner —how would you do it? How would it look; orderly or spontaneous? Having things decided or leaving them open-ended? Completing a task early or finishing it at the last minute?

Remember the vacation story of my friends Veronica and Craig? As a reminder, they were the ones who could not agree about the specific day that golf would be played while on vacation. Veronica, the *5 o'clock-sharp* person, wanted the golf date to be planned and confirmed. In contrast, Craig, as the *5 o'clock-somewhere* person, sought to leave the date open-ended to maintain flexibility. By the way, neither of these styles is right or wrong…they are simply different.

People in the *5 o'clock-sharp* group are decisive, organized and prefer to plan things out. These individuals are quite methodical and systematic in their approach to life. If there is a school, community, or business project due, you can count on them to have their part done before the deadline. They schedule their time accordingly to allow for unexpected circumstances. For them, anxiety occurs when things are left undecided. They operate by the expression, "plan your work and work your plan."

On the other hand, people in the *5 o'clock-somewhere* group are flexible, casual and spontaneous in their actions. Moreover, they seek to "go with the flow." These individuals are creative in their approach to life and thrive on adapting and changing course, as need be, along the way. A project will likely be completed by the final due date but generally with no time to spare.

Why would they do this? It is simple. This group actually thrives on doing things at the last minute. They get anxious when too many things are scheduled in advance and obtain their energy from the last minute rush of meeting a deadline. They operate by the expression "work until you determine a plan and then follow it until a better plan develops."

We all move between these two groups. However, we all have a definite preference in regard to how we plan our time and lives.

In order to help identify your default style, I have listed some questions for you to consider.

1. When you first arrive at the beach condo on vacation, would you rather go for a walk on the beach or unpack and organize all of your clothes? (unpack = *5 o'clock-sharp*, walk on beach = *5 o'clock-somewhere*)

2. Do you keep your car neat/organized or is it messy/unorganized? (neat/organized = *5 o'clock-sharp*, messy/unorganized = *5 o'clock- somewhere*)

3. When grocery shopping, do you prefer to write things you need on a list and go through the store in a methodical way or do you prefer to buy what you need (no list needed) and go through the aisles in a random manner? (make a list/methodical = *5 o'clock-sharp*, no list needed/random manner = *5 o'clock-somewhere*)

4. Do you prefer making your New Year's Eve plans one month in advance or a few days before the big night? (one month in advance = *5 o'clock-sharp*, few days before = *5 o'clock-somewhere*)

5. If you had a choice between someone giving you a lot with a mountain view or one with a beach view, would you immediately decide which lot you wanted or would you seek to keep your options open and get back to them? (decide immediately = *5 o'clock-sharp*, keep your options open = *5 o'clock-somewhere*)

6. If you are going on a long drive, do you prefer to decide which hotel you will stop at in advance or to find a hotel to stop at when you get tired of driving? (decide in advance

= *5 o'clock-sharp*, find a hotel when tired = *5 o'clock-somewhere*)

7. Do you prefer to receive a gift card as a birthday present so you can use it when and how you want or a tangible present as a birthday gift that you can use now? (gift you can use now = *5 o'clock-sharp*, gift card to use when you want = *5 o'clock-somewhere*)

As stated before, it is vital when learning adaptive communications not only to understand our own styles but also the preferences of those with whom we communicate. Through such understanding, we can adapt our communications as needed to be most effective.

Here are some ways to determine what group another person is part of.

1. Does the PTA president of the local high school push to get things decided or patiently listen to others and let ideas slowly develop? (rush to get things decided = *5 o'clock-sharp*, patiently listen to others = *5 o'clock-somewhere*)

2. Is your boss frustrated when a client's problem cannot be solved immediately or content with the concept that some client problems tend to work themselves out over time? (frustrated that a problem can't be solved quickly = *5 o'clock-sharp*, content to let problem work out over time = *5 o'clock-somewhere*)

3. Is the father at your kid's soccer game into the action and cheering on his child/team, or is he glancing at his watch to see if the game is almost over? (glancing at his watch = *5 o'clock-sharp*, into the action = *5 o'clock-somewhere*)

4. When going to dinner with your friend, does she know exactly where she wants to go eat or does she have a hard

time deciding? (knows where she wants to go = *5 o'clock-sharp*, hard time deciding = *5 o'clock-somewhere*)

5. When going to eat at your favorite restaurant, does your father know what he will order before he gets there, or does he prefer to wait until the last minute to see what sounds best? (knows what he will order = *5 o'clock-sharp*, wait and see what sounds best = *5 o'clock-somewhere*)

These are just a few ways to help you determine another person's *5 o'clock-sharp* versus *5 o'clock-somewhere* preference. There are many other questions to consider but this gives you some tangible ways to determine a person's style. The important thing is to make an assessment and determine the other person's preference so you can then communicate more effectively.

Let's look at the following scenario between two coworkers. Here is a conversation that takes place between a *5 o'clock-sharp* person (Jason) and a *5 o'clock-somewhere* person (Scott).

Jason asks, "Where do you want to go for lunch?"

Scott says, "I don't know, but I guess anything is fine."

Jason replies, "Ok, then, let's go to the seafood restaurant."

What happens here is something we all have seen. What Scott really means, when he says "I don't know…anything is fine" is that he has not yet decided what he wants and does not like being pushed to make a decision. On the other hand, Jason, who seeks to get the lunch destination decided, takes Scott's reply at face value and quickly makes the lunch decision for them. In turn, Scott sees Jason as controlling and Jason views Scott as being indecisive.

If they used *adaptive communications* and knew each other's styles this conversation would have sounded different. Here is an example.

Jason says, "Scott, what might sound good for lunch today—pizza, seafood or a sandwich? Do any of these sound good?"

Scott says, "Pizza sounds great."

Jason says, "Do you want to go to Ernie's Pizza or Diane's Pizzeria?"

Scott says, "Man they are both good, but let's go to Diane's."

Jason says, "Sounds good and we are on the way."

So, in this second scenario Jason met Scott's communications needs. He adapted his own *5 o'clock-sharp* style to Scott's *5'o clock-somewhere* preference. In this second scenario, Jason was fine with pizza, seafood or sandwiches. By giving Scott three choices, however, he was able to meet Scott's needs of making a decision on his own and avoid coming across in a "controlling manner." Scott appreciated the options and saw that Jason was really interested in what he wanted to eat.

Here are some strategies for adapting your *5 o'clock-sharp* style to someone's *5 o'clock-somewhere* type:

- Give them time to make a decision.

- Loosen up your demeanor, and relax your approach.

- Expect and prepare for a lot of questions from them.

- Provide them with options from which to choose.

- Spend time focusing on the process of making the decision, not simply the decision itself.

Strategies for adapting your *5 o'clock-somewhere* style to someone's *5'o clock-sharp* style:

- Always arrive early for any meeting/encounter.

- Be clear in what you say and decisive in your explanation.

- Come prepared so that you do not waste time.

- Give them choices so they can "make the decision."

- Come to a mutually beneficially conclusion, and do not leave things unresolved.

Well…we did it. We have gone through all four components of the *Adaptive Communications* model. We spent time discussing four prominent and contrasting types of communications that are the backbone of the *Everyone Is in Sales* mindset. I recommend reading and then re-reading these chapters. Also, human beings are not robots and no person is always a "this" or "that." When reading the descriptions, your goal is to decide (between the two) which one is most like you and most like another.

We all have some of these tendencies, but one will always be more preferred to us than the other. Again, think *right-hand vs. left-hand*. One of them is generally easier for you to use. It is the same thing here. Also, remember when these different components are blended together, you end up with many unique personality types.

In addition, life circumstances, stress, relationships we are in, family, our job, business, health, age, and many other factors impact our natural styles. With that said, if you begin to embrace adaptive communications, you will be able to identify how you and others prefer to communicate. This makes for much better communications and thus a better life.

We will now move on to Section III of the book that addresses how integrated communications (online and offline) work, and what this means to our communications efforts. Or, said another way, what we need to think about in regard to our communications—as we seek to further embrace the *Everyone Is in Sales* philosophy.

SECTION III

Integrated Communications

CHAPTER 10

Integrating Social Media into the Real World

We hear about social media all the time. For example, *connect* with me on LinkedIn...*like us* on facebook or *follow us* on Twitter. OK, you get the idea. But, whether you are a veteran or newbie to social media there are some things I want you to consider.

Social media is simple. It is *a tool* not *the tool* in your overall communications mix. In my consulting work, I have seen far too many organizations try and implement social media as some kind of "silver bullet" strategy that will cure their business woes. It simply does not work this way. Like any other communications or business strategy, it takes methodical implementation. So if you are in this group, I am sorry to break the bad news, but it is vital that you understand this.

> *Social media is simple. It is a tool not the tool in your overall communications mix.*

In addition, it is easy to forget that in our online, all-the-time world, social media is only one of many methods of communications available to us. The other ones never went away. Social media, much like websites when they first came out, have changed the way we communicate, and it is simply one of the newest ways to communicate.

Whether you ultimately love, like, tolerate or hate social media, I encourage you to take time to truly understand it. Why? It is important. There is a fundamental shift taking place in the way human beings communicate. This was the reason I embraced it. This book focuses on communications, so it makes logical sense to understand what these changes mean to us.

Social media is the great equalizer. It allows any person around the globe—no matter their race, gender, age, status or nationality—to have an unfiltered voice and to express their opinion. In other words, they can influence others. My friend and colleague Mark W. Schaefer (who wrote the foreword of this book) addresses this topic further in his book *Return on Influence*.

So, the entire idea of social media is quite simple: it allows human beings to communicate in a new way. Within the scope of social media, I am including not only things such as facebook, Twitter, LinkedIn, and YouTube, but also mobile media such as text messaging. You may think that this type of communications is a fad and only for young kids. Maybe you think it will go away. Not so! To many, *texting* is *talking*!

Recently, my oldest daughter told me to give her and her friend some space when we got outside the restaurant. I asked why. She said they needed to talk privately. I said, "No problem." However, I was astonished to see the two of them standing shoulder to shoulder on a wall outside the restaurant and "texting" each other what they needed to say. You may think I am kidding...I am not!

I encourage you to be open minded as we explore these new types of communications—they are here to stay. And, yes, while there are some negatives that come with these new mediums, I argue that the positive attributes far outweigh any negative ones.

Here is an interesting dichotomy to consider. Our world moves at a faster pace and is more global than ever; however, simultaneously our world has become smaller—news spreads across the globe in minutes. Just think of the news we received in a "real time" manner through social media channels regarding the revolt that was occurring in Egypt. Another example was the details we learned—almost instantly through social media—regarding the earthquake in Haiti. Social media made us feel the pain of these events as they were happening.

These types of communications did not exist even a decade ago when 9-11 occurred. They have changed everything. Social media allows us to connect with people across the globe that we would otherwise never know, and more importantly, to develop meaningful real world relationships with them. I will say it time and time again—it is all about communications and all about people.

So how do I define social media? It is about two-way communications. It's about community. It's about connections. It's about conversations. It's about dialogue. In this world where we all move so fast, it provides a new way to meet people and build meaningful relationships with them.

There are disturbing aspects to this new method of communications that must be considered. We have all—no matter our age—come to rely on emails, texting, social media and other methods of "impersonal communications" a great deal. It is happening to such an extent that I am seeing firsthand—as a professor in university classrooms and as a consultant—that many people are losing the ability to have real-life/real-time conversations. In addition, everyone's attention span (all ages) seems to be getting increasingly shorter.

As an example, about a year ago, I was helping interview some college graduates for an organization's customer service opening. The first method I used in the interview process was to determine how the candidates expressed themselves through the written word. So, I emailed each of the top candidates a handful of questions to answer. Overall, the answers were OK. However, there was no way to know who actually answered the questions or who proofed their writing.

So I moved on to the next step—the phone interview. I began with my friendly style, and the candidates quickly relaxed. First, I asked them some easy questions—such as their favorite type of boss, their strengths and weaknesses etc. Their answers were "textbook and rehearsed" in nature. This is what I expected. So, to get them away from their pre-planned responses, I threw each of them a curveball question. The question was simple in nature, but left them speechless. I asked each of them, "What do you like better; apples or oranges, and why?" I could sense the stress at the other end of the phone line. They all asked, "What do you mean? What are you looking for?" I simply replied, "You do know what apples and oranges are—right? Which do you like better and why?"

Again, there was just silence as each person tried to think of an answer. When they began talking, they stumbled all over themselves trying to provide some meaningful answer. Bottom line, they did not answer my question and did not reply logically…and I walked away quite concerned about their ability to "think on their feet." These candidates expected a certain set of questions and had prepared to answer them. When I asked questions that they were unprepared for, they simply had no adequate response.

This made me realize that younger generations particularly—but all of us to some degree—have become accustomed to receiving information when we want it and how we want it (think DVR and no commercials). We choose to respond to others when we want and how we want. So, it is of vital importance that we don't lose our ability to communicate in traditional ways while embracing these new communications mediums.

The ability to communicate effectively on the phone and in person is quickly becoming a lost art. Those who work hard at this skill, in addition to embracing the new methods, will have a great advantage in every part of life. When our interactions are real-life/real-time, we are not able to respond *when we feel like it*, or ponder something a day or so before hitting *reply*. We must be able to communicate immediately and effectively. So, as this chapter covers social media and the real world, I stress that this phenomenon is one we must all take seriously.

My biggest concern over the use of social media is that it negatively impacts our ability to communicate in the "real world." I have students who simply hate talking in front of small groups (who said they previously had no problem with it) and others who write their papers using expressions that include *LOL* as part of a sentence. Does this mean I am blaming all of the changes in communications on social media? Of course not, however, it does play a role in influencing these habits.

Another issue I see with the vast amount of texts, emails, and tweets, is that many people are losing their ability to use good grammar and correct spelling when writing. For example, I had a student tell me that I should not count off for his misspelling. He said it was unfair for me to do so, since he had run his paper through spell check…twice. I thought he was kidding. (I know you hope I am kidding.) Sorry—I am not, and this is true! For him, the automated function of the computer eliminated his need to check his own work. He truly felt the computer was designed to correct his errors.

I grew up around a traditional newspaper publishing business, helped run a printing business for many years and have recently embraced social media and more. So, you may ask, do I love social media? No. Do I like it? Yes. Do I love any type of media? No. Do I like many types of media? Yes. To me all of the communications mediums have their place, but they are not truly effective alone. The magic happens when they are all integrated together. So, do I love integrated communications? Absolutely.

Good communications—even using social media—is all about adapting your method and style of communications (remember the last section of the book) to meet the needs of the person you are communicating with. I recommend that you first consider what medium you prefer to communicate through. Do you know? In other words what is your natural preference or choice to use in a particular situation?

Do you like to meet in person, talk on the phone, receive an email, receive a handwritten note, or communicate via facebook? Do you know your friends, families, business associates and customers preferred methods of communicating? If not—as I stress to clients all the time—ask them. If they like to talk on the phone, adapt your style and call them. If they prefer a text message, adapt your style and text them. Again, remember all that we covered in Section II and the *adaptive communications* model. If they prefer receiving a hard-copy letter, then adapt your style and mail them a letter. If they prefer meeting in person, then adapt your style and meet them in person. The whole idea is to adapt your communications methods to best meet the needs of the person you are communicating with.

So, what is social media about? It is about having conversations. However, it is not about getting on facebook, Twitter, or LinkedIn and talking about how great you are. It is just like real life—the goal is listening to others and engaging them in meaningful dialogue. Listen first and talk second.

Let's think about it another way. If you go to a neighborhood party, do you seek to have a meaningful two-way conversation with others (remember communications with an "s") or do you prefer having someone communicate "at you" and never take a real interest in you/listen to you? I think most of us seek out the conversations where we are truly listened to and there is give and take in the conversation. Such conversations are the ones that meet our needs and that we find most enjoyable.

Is this not similar to the Golden Rule? The Golden Rule states that we are to treat others the same way we wish to be treated. So we must remember that social media is no different than real world encounters. We should communicate with others in the way we want to be communicated with.

So, if you like to be heard, then listen to others. If you like to be understood then affirm others. If you like people to show a genuine interest in you, then show a true interest in them. If you don't like people to interrupt you when you are speaking, then don't cut them off when they are talking. You see…it is quite simple, and we all know these things on some level. Furthermore, we all learned these things as young children, but many of us have developed bad habits over the years.

What you text, tweet, post, blog and otherwise send out through social media becomes your style or brand of communications. There is a chapter on this later in the book. What you communicate through these mediums is your philosophy of human relations. However, in the new age of communications, it is open for the world to see. I suggest you think of social media as being your digital tattoo, because everything you do is visible to the world, is always with you, never goes away, and influences how others view you in "offline" settings.

So what are the unique challenges of social media? Let's start with the basic ones:

- It can be impersonal.

- It can seem overwhelming.

- It can be annoying.

- It can be distracting.

- It can provide information to you that you simply do not want to know.

- It can be rude.

Here is a good example. How many people do you see "looking down" at their mobile device as you pass them in the mall or airport? My unscientific estimate is about two-thirds of the people are doing this. I give a speech entitled *Leaders Look Up,* and it questions if we are becoming a society of people who are looking down.

Furthermore, many people are missing the present world they physically inhabit and instead are being entertained by a virtual world that is not in front of them. For example, how many people look at their smart phones before going to sleep—the last thing they do each night—and look at them again the first thing upon waking up? From my research, I have determined that many people do this. Moreover, many people sleep with their phones. Wow, I hope they are not used as a pillow.

Here is another story. I recently took my two youngest daughters to an animated kid's movie. My four-year-old began asking me—20 minutes into the movie—how much longer the movie would last. She told me she was bored and asked if she could play games on my phone. Wow...this shocked me! For me, movies have always been both an escape and entertainment, but to her (in our information overloaded world) a movie was not even engaging. What does this mean to our future generations? Only time will tell.

There is an important place in our world for social media; however, it can never replace real life, present, and personal communications. OK, you may have guessed it...I believe in the power of real world relationships. After all human beings are designed to have relationships (in person) not to become "virtual" robots. This is important for us to remember.

So, if you are a person who spends more time looking at your facebook feed—while at dinner with a date—than talking to the other person you are with, stop and put the phone down! This is rude. I am not judging you—I struggle with the same issue. I get caught up in looking at this "magic device" as well... but it is not polite. My writing this in a book will give my wife great enjoyment—when reminding me of this—when I "forget" my own advice.

Remember that there is an evolving etiquette to using these tools, and there are times to use them and times when we should not. For example, never—and please I am begging you—use your mobile device while in the restroom. I wish I was kidding.

We all need to remember to be present in the moment and turn off the social media noise at specific times each day. Don't worry; it will be waiting for you when you turn it back on. I promise you, if you let it, that these tools will occupy every waking hour of your day. You must set boundaries of how, when and why you are going to use these tools. Be purposeful, deliberate and intentional in your choices.

Before you send that tweet, facebook message, email or text to someone, always ask yourslf if it would be more effective (though not as fast) to take a little more time and communicate though a better and more traditional channel. Again, no amount of LOL, smiley faces, J/K or other such expressions/icons can make up for the personal touch.

Human beings have a tone in their voice and an expression in their face and body. None of this is visible in social media. All people can see are icons, avatars and text. So when you are using social media, be as real and down to earth as possible. Be sure to carefully choose your words, tone and sentence structure. And, always take a moment to reflect before hitting *send*. Doing these things ensures that your message can be easily understood and achieve the kind of response you want. In other words, use *adaptive communications* when using social media to best meet the needs of your audience.

It is important to remember that the written word—no matter how it is delivered—has a life of its own. It is like that digital tattoo I mentioned before. I can give you countless examples of people who have written a statement on Twitter, facebook, or LinkedIn and then taken it down minutes later. Guess what?— too late. Whatever you have written is there to stay.

There are three important concepts to ponder as you use social media:

1. You should consider everything you write as if you were sending a BCC (Blind Carbon Copy) email to the world. So, if you have no problem with what you have written being shared all over the globe, then write it. If you are not sure, then reflect further before submitting.

2. Have a social media purpose. You should always seek to understand others and help them, promote them etc. before asking for anything.

3. Be authentic and transparent in your posts. Social media embraces those who are "real people" and shuns those who are full of themselves and/or are trying to hard sell something.

If you go to a networking event, do you want to spend time with the "hard-sell and death-grip" handshake guy? You know the guy who refuses to quit pitching you on how great his company, services and offerings are. Of course you don't.

We are all looking (online or offline) to build relationships with people we trust. And, trust is a huge component of social media. Aren't we much more responsive to a person who politely walks up and asks us about ourselves? Of course we are. These people say little about themselves or their company, because their goal is to build a relationship with us, not "close a deal." The same is true in social media. If you go around promoting yourself, blasting others, hard selling how great your offerings are…guess what? Few people will listen or care.

Social media has its limitations. Is it the right choice of communications sometime? Yes. Is it the right communications choice all the time? No. Remember to think through what it is you seek to communicate. Always ask yourself how your tone may come across, and if this is a message the receiver will understand. The traditional model of communications was quite simple. You had a sender, receiver, a message, a feedback loop and noise. Now, there are many more ways to communicate and there is much more noise. We covered this early in the book.

As a personal example, here are some of the ways that I receive and exchange information:

- **Traditional mail:** (2) I have a physical home address and business address where mail is sent.

- **Email:** (6) I have six emails: my personal email, two business emails, my doctoral studies email, my professor email from one university and my professor email from a second university.

- **Facebook personal page:** (2) On my personal FB account, I get messages sent to me privately and also get messages sent to me publicly.

- **Facebook Business page:** (1) I get messages posted to me on our wall.

- **LinkedIn:** (2) I get private messages sent to me directly from people I am connected with, and I get messages from those who are in my LinkedIn Groups.

- **Text messages:** (1) I get text messages to my cell phone.

- **Phone calls:** (3) I get calls to my office phone, cell phone, and home phone number.

- **Twitter:** (2) I get private messages (DM) sent to me and public messages to me via my Twitter account.

- **Voicemail:** (3) I get messages left for me on my cell phone, my work phone and my home phone.

- **Blog:** (1) I get responses to the blog posts I write.

OK—and I am sure I am missing some—but if you count this up, I have 23+ ways that information is *frequently* shared with me. This sounds crazy, but when I talk with most people using new technologies, they also are trying to find a way to keep up with all of these communications channels.

This is why we hear expressions such as, "I am drowning, I am swamped, I am buried, I am running ragged, I am slammed, I am covered up" ...and the list goes on. By the way, none of these expressions sound good—right? One reason for this type of negative response is that simply keeping up with email, voicemail and hard mail was already time consuming. Now it is nearly impossible. I consider social media to be "email on steroids" as it never stops. Ever! It can be totally overwhelming, so please take this chapter into consideration if you embrace social media in your communications efforts. For me, there are only two choices with social media. You must either embrace it completely or not do it at all. It is really bad to do social media "half way."

So, what do you do? First, you must realize that you cannot respond to all of the messages immediately. They are not all of equal importance, nor do they require the same response time. You must operate from what I call "last things last" mindset and let people know your normal response time. For example, a message you receive through LinkedIn may take you longer to respond to than a text message. So, always set realistic expectations. Also, let people know your preferred method to receive communications. For example, if you would rather talk on the phone than get a facebook message, let people know that. Again, remember to focus on the least pressing issue last!

Here are some things to consider:

- Are you sending a "one-way communication style" text or email to deliver news that could best be communicated with a "two-way communications" phone call?

- Are you writing a post on your friend's facebook wall about a private matter that would be more effective in a face-to-face conversation?

These are things we must think about. The magic of social media occurs when "online" connections become real life friendships. Let me tell you a story about how this is working for me.

When I began actively using Twitter, I began to follow a person named Kent Huffman who lived in Texas (by the way, to illustrate the power of this, his testimonial is in the front of this book). Kent created lists to keep track of the top marketing leaders on Twitter. I was included in his list. Wow, Kent hooked me...and I was impressed. After all, Everyone Is in Sales, right?

Well, when I knew I was going on a business trip to Dallas, I contacted Kent to see if we could get together in real life. We were able to do this and met for dinner while I was in town. We immediately struck up a friendship. Kent told me of some of his future plans, and he became a client of mine as well. So who says social media has no (ROI) return on investment?

A couple of months later, I learned that Kent, had given my name to a great guy in Canada named Jeff Ashcroft who was starting a group known as the Social CMO. Jeff's idea was to bring together top creative, public relations, and marketing minds from traditional mediums that had generated a strong following/ presence in social media. So based on Kent's referral, Jeff and I connected via phone. Jeff and and I became fast friends too, and I became a member of the Social CMO group. (For more: thesocialcmo.com)

Once the group was established, we began talking about getting together in person. One member of the group, Amy Howell in Memphis, TN, who runs her own PR/Marketing firm, made something happen. (Oh, before I forget, for those of you still discounting the value of social media, Amy also wrote a testimonial for this book that is inside the front cover.) Amy brought social media guru Chris Brogan into town to speak and pulled together our first-ever meeting. Before this meeting, I called Amy, who at this time I only knew thru social media. We talked on the phone for a long time. Amy also has become a friend.

PAUSE...are you seeing that social media is about building relationships and that everyone ultimately wants to meet in real life (or *IRL* as the abbreviation goes)?

OK...UNPAUSE...

While on the phone with Amy, she asked me if I knew another Atlanta resident with whom she had been communicating in social media named Billy Mitchell. I told her no, and she suggested that I track him down. And, I did. It turned out that Billy Mitchell ran a successful creative and marketing firm just three miles from my office. In addition his home was located only a few miles from my home. Wow, right? So, I quickly connected with Billy, and we became friends. Billy and his company, MLT Creative, became clients and partners of mine. They are top notch.

When I went to Memphis for the first Social CMO group meeting, I developed new (real life) friends in addition to the ones listed above such as Jeremy Victor, Glen Gilmore, Mark Schaefer, Deb Weinstein, Anne Gallaher (back cover testimonial), the late Trey Pennington, Eric Fletcher, Alex Romanovich, Kathy Snavely , Chris Brogan and many more.

About nine months later, the group decided that we needed to do a follow-up event in another city. This new meeting, under Mark Schaefer's (foreword) leadership, became the ultra-successful Social Slam conference. For those of you who know Twitter #soslam.

Through an organic movement that was promoted primarily through social media, the attendees topped 500, and people had to be turned away. I should have scalped some tickets—yes it was that big! Some were scalping tickets. Oh yeah...social media is just a fad, right? OK... just kidding.

At this event, not only did I speak and gain new clients but met new friends such as Jay Baer, CK Kerley, Laura Click, Dan Christ and Alan Brocious. This event triggered my friend Anne Gallaher along with Dan Christ, Alan Brocious and Stephanie Gehman,

Kathy Snavely and others in Harrisburg, PA, to put on their own conference called Social Media at Work. *(For you Twitter lovers that hashtag is #smatwork.) As a result of my speaking at the Harrisburg conference, I made many new contacts, gained a new client, and hired a new vendor. And...the story is continuing as I type this...*

This is a long story, but here is the point. Social media is about being social. It gives us an unprecedented opportunity to connect with people online and then create real life personal relationships with them. Here is the most important thing I want you to remember in thinking about communications and social media: Each one of us enjoyed connecting in real life far more than chatting online. Why? Because we are all human beings and were created to spend time with each other.

So, as you can see, the series of connections I have covered ties many parts of North America together both "online and offline," and shows how new friendships were built. This is why I spend time in social media. Trust me...I am not a "computer guy." As a matter of fact computers seem to break when I get too close to them.

In all seriousness, social media is a way to connect with others who you would never have otherwise connected with. And, it is about building relationships that are very powerful! Trust me, the ROI you are looking for pays off in dollars, but far more in terms of quality relationships. So, never lose sight of the powerful human relationships that develop through social media.

If done right, social media is a lot more than buzz, hype and talking. In contrast, it is a fundamental shift in human communications. I hope you take time to relook at this channel of communications in a strategic manner as it can add value to your business, life and more. Remember, it is a communications channel that is here to stay. The names of facebook, Twitter, LinkedIn, etc. may indeed change, but the new ways in which we can communicate "one to one" and "one to many" are here to stay.

Now we will move on and discuss what I call *The 5 C's of Effective Communications*. They are important in online and offline settings. They are vital to successful integrated communications. So, we have a few more chapters to go. Stay with me—you will be glad you did.

CHAPTER 11

The 5 C's of Effective Communications

In the last chapter, we discussed the importance of social media and what it *really* means. In doing so, we covered the good, the bad and the ugly. More importantly, we addressed how it affects our world, and how we must endeavor to deliberately blend our online and offline communications.

This section of the book focuses on integrated communications, and we are going to look at another model—one that applies to our overall communications efforts. *The 5 C's of Effective Communications* focuses on five key aspects of communications. The 5 C's are: **clarity, consistency, content, connection and creativity**. If we can remember these five concepts, they will help us become better communicators in every aspect of life.

> *The 5 C's are: clarity, consistency, content, connection and creativity.*

1. Clarity

The first C is *clarity*. How often have we heard someone say, "Let me be crystal clear about this?" When people say this, it is usually because they are frustrated or feel others don't understand what they are saying. Someone who is getting ready to give important instructions to a person or to a group often says, "Let me be *clear* about what I am going to say here." Here is another example: "Let me be sure you are hearing me loud and *clear*." The word *clear* is used (for our purposes) interchangeably with the word *clarity*.

In all of these examples, the person who is communicating first indicates emphatically that what they are about to say is important, thus ensuring that the other party is engaged. The person communicating seeks clarity in the interaction. Maybe, their goal is to ensure the other party pays "extra attention" to the concepts that are being conveyed or will be conveyed. Here is what this means to us: the words we use—whether verbal or written in nature—must be straightforward and precise. They can't be ambiguous; they must provide clarity.

For example, if you are seeking to communicate urgency, the choice of words you use is of utmost importance. You should use the expression, "I need it now," not "I need it soon." Read the two of them again, and note the distinction. You will see they are similar but much different in intent. "Soon" is open-ended and unclear; whereas, "now" clearly and unequivocally means immediately.

Likewise, if you need something turned in by 5 p.m. on Thursday; you must be precise and clear. You can't tell another person to "turn it in ASAP." By the way, *ASAP* (as soon as possible) is vague and means nothing to another person. Think about the expression. *As soon as possible*, or *ASAP*, as I have learned over the years, means the other person will get it turned in to you as soon as it is possible/feasible for them (to have time etc.) to do so. So, not indicating a specific time and date creates a lack of clarity.

Again, if you want to drive someone to a specific action, tell them exactly what it is you want them to do. Do not create ambiguity by saying, "Would you mind doing this?" In contrast, be certain your words are not confusing and ensure your syntax is appropriate for the situation. In addition, be sure both the tone of your voice and your body language correspond with the words you use.

If you are online (where tone and body expression do not exist) you must be even more careful and deliberate. In such cases, use extra phrases such as, "It was a pleasure to talk to you earlier," or "Thanks so much for your time." Such expressions convey a pleasant tone. Also, be certain—before communicating anything—what your intent is; and what you are specifically hoping to accomplish. Do you know? If not, you need to determine this so you can communicate more effectively and provide optimal clarity in your message.

2. Consistency

The second C is *consistency*. The overall consistency of our communications is quite important. We can't merely talk the talk; we must *walk* the talk consistently. We cannot do one thing and say another, nor can we compartmentalize our lives. Furthermore, we cannot behave in one fashion with one group of people and in an opposite manner with a different group. This is inconsistent behavior. For example, inconsistent communications occur when you talk to one person and stress how religious you are and that you hate profanity. However, when talking to another person, in a different setting, you use a great deal of profanity. This is inconsistent communications and this is not good. Consistent communications occur when you communicate the same message and reflect the same values no matter who the audience is or what medium you are using.

Our consistent communications define who we are. This means, whether we are in a personal or professional setting, whether we are blogging or talking to a group, whether we are on facebook or LinkedIn, or whether we are at our job or our kid's football game, it is vital that our communications be consistent and not contradictory.

What message do you seek to communicate to the world? Once you have thought through this—or perhaps you already know—create an integrated strategy to communicate this consistent message in every component of your life. Consistency means that your choice of clothes, car you drive, job you have, words you use, friends you keep, and more are compatible and in alignment.

Such actions ensure that others view you in an authentic, genuine, and reliable manner. In contrast, inconsistent communications cause people to see you in the opposite manner. Again, in every aspect (online and offline) of your life—work diligently to ensure your communications are consistent.

3. Content

The third C is *content*. Good content is vital to successful communications. So remember this simple equation: Good content = good communications. You see, it does not matter how much or how little you communicate if your content is lacking. When what you communicate lacks value—regardless of how great your style or delivery might be—no one really wants to listen to you.

Therefore, it is all about providing valuable content in your communications. For example, you may have a blog that is search engine optimized (SEO) and well designed. However, if it lacks compelling content, nobody will actively seek to read it. If you have a blog that has an "OK" design and little SEO, but offers great content, people will seek you out and read your stuff. Trust me.

Human beings desire to learn something or be captivated by a new idea when engaging in the communications process. This is where good content comes in. It allows you to provide a fresh perspective. Good content demands attention and gets it. People do not invest time following or engaging with someone who lacks good content.

People who provide valuable content in their communications provide both the "steak and the sizzle" that others desire. Think of content as being a good steak. All the hype in the world and/ or marketing of the steak will not be effective if the steak itself is inferior. The same holds true with our content. So, always provide great information and value in all your communications.

4. Connection

The fourth C is *connection*. Human beings inherently need to connect. You see, we all have a natural desire to collaborate with others. And, yes, that goes for people who prefer spending time alone, talking less, and reflecting more—as we discussed in the adaptive communications section of this book. We all desire to be part of something bigger than ourselves. We seek to have a conversation.

There are countless examples of this. Think of the great number of young people who volunteered to help with Barack Obama's 2008 presidential campaign. He sought to bring about change, and they connected with his message. Others identify with their college football team or the fraternity/sorority they were in. Some people have their need for connection met by joining the local country club, their neighborhood association, or the PTA at their kids' schools.

Connections are important because they center on personal relationships. And, as we all know, strong relationships are the backbone of solid communications. I recommend that you find ways in all of your communications to connect with others. What areas and interests do you have in common? Sports? Travel? Reading? You get the idea.

Also, find opportunities to promote and "connect" your friends and colleagues from various parts of your life. Be deliberate about trying to refer people you know to one another. Always recommend the work that another person has done for you to people in your circle of influence. This manner of helping others goes a long way in building stronger relationships and developing connections.

In short, be in the "business" of connecting people. It is unfortunate that we often get so focused on promoting ourselves and/ or our own initiatives that we miss the opportunity to help others. So, remember the fourth C, connection, is about relationships. It is about conversations. It is about having a dialogue and about collaborating with others in an effective manner.

5. Creativity

The fifth C is *creativity*. Remember your parents telling you, "It's not just what you say but also how you say it that matters?" This is still great advice. This statement applies to creativity. Two people can both convey the same overall concept; however, the one with the most creative approach will be most effective in their communications of the concept.

Creativity at work is something that is incredible to observe. For instance, I have seen some students in my university classes present on a topic and make the presentation incredibly creative. In contrast, I have seen other students present on the identical topic, and the presentation comes off as dry and uneventful. So, why were some of them more creative? Why does this matter? Well, first it allowed the creative ones to communicate better than the others. They provided their content (yes, one of the 5 C's) in a fresh, thought-provoking, and inspirational way. They engaged their audience. In short, their creativity made them the better communicators.

You see, they put a new twist on a traditional concept and expressed it in a fresh and relevant way. Our creativity is the component that enables us to do things in an original manner. Creativity is about doing something remarkable and distinctly memorable. Creativity is about thinking of things in a new way. Such creativity allows each person to be unique in their communications. This uniqueness allows a person's message to be remembered and for it to stand out from the crowd.

For the most part, there is no such thing as a new idea—every idea is generally one that is borrowed or built upon an existing one. I do a lot of speaking engagements. What is it about me or another presenter that makes a presentation different—assuming that the content is the same? The answer is creativity. My creative approach—or that of another presenter—is what makes such presentations memorable, unique, engaging, or—if done well—remarkable.

If most people "zig" in their style of communications (the norm), I challenge you to "zag" (not the norm) in your communications style—be original and show more creativity. This fifth component of the 5 C's of Effective Communications is powerful. Creative people go further. Creative people are not afraid to challenge the status quo. In short, creative people are effective communicators.

Utilizing the 5 C's model (*clarity, consistency, content, connection* and *creativity*) helps us to become better communicators. So let's review…

- First, remember to provide **clarity** in all that you communicate. The clearer you are in your communications; the more successful you will be.

- Second, always be **consistent** in what you say, write and do. Great communicators and thus those who are most successful in life are consistent and "walk the talk."

- Third, always provide valuable **content**. So, if you are writing an email or talking to a friend, make sure the information you are sharing is valuable.

- Fourth, remember that all human beings desire a *connection*. Help connect others together and find ways to meet new people.

- Fifth, be *creative* and look to take a new or existing idea and make it your own. You cannot create every new idea, but you can be creative in how you approach them and life itself. Great communicators are creative in their approach.

When you incorporate the 5 C's model into your everyday life, you will maximize the effectiveness of your communications. This impacts how we interact with groups, which will be covered in the next chapter.

CHAPTER 12

Communications and Group Dynamics

In previous chapters we have focused on individual communications preferences. However, much of our communications take place in group settings; thus, we will look at how to communicate with a group more effectively. Groups come together for a specific reason, and consequently they have a specific style of communications that needs to be considered. When we are communicating to a group, it requires a different strategy since there are more people involved in the process. The equation is quite simple: the more people in the group, the more complex the communications strategy. Let's explore how we can become better communicators in group settings.

> *It is key that we examine and identify a group's current developmental stage so that we can communicate appropriately and effectively.*

To best understand how groups develop, I am going to share a model that was developed by Bruce Tuckman. Group development generally falls into one of four stages: *Forming, Storming, Norming and Performing*. It is key that we examine and identify a group's current developmental stage so that we can communicate appropriately and effectively. Each stage has defining characteristics that we must learn to identify.

In the *forming* stage, the members of a group are new to each other, and the group is in the early part of its development. In this stage, there is generally a lot of confusion, unclear objectives, and a lack of listening. We must keep this in mind when communicating with them. For instance, in this stage of of development, a group will require more guidance from us since they are not yet accustomed to working together. In addition, these groups will require specific recommendations from us that are both concise and clear in nature. It is important that we not add to the confusion of the new group—as there is enough of it already going on in this stage.

In the *storming* stage, members of the group have worked together for a while. However, in this stage, they are still trying to "hammer out" what the focus of their group will be and what its structure will be. It is common in this stage to observe arguments, anger, inconsistency and the presence of hidden agendas. This stage requires us to communicate to them "what can be" and paint a vision of the future. In addition, in this stage, the group has yet to come to a consensus regarding how decisions are made. So as communicators, we must "tread carefully"—give particular attention to what we say, how we say it, when we say it, and whom we assume to be the "leader" of the group. All of this is still developing in this stage.

In the *norming* stage, the group is finally beginning to figure out who they want to be. At this point, things start to become standardized and the overall listening improves. Moreover, the group is able to logically assess its strengths and weaknesses. In this stage, the group has been together long enough that the members have become quite similar in nature. Thus, when communicating with this stage group, we must remember that they are more developed and mature as well as more logical and standardized in their decision making.

In the **performing** stage, the group has become effective. The team is cohesive. Goals are met, creativity is exhibited, people know what to expect from each other, and thus confidence, morale and success are high. In this stage, groups are "well-oiled machines" that operate both efficiently and effectively. As communicators, we must seek to determine who the "leaders" (whether formal or informal) are within the group. Furthermore, we must carefully plan out what our communications strategy will be. We know that this stage group tends to make consistent and similar decisions over time. Thus, we must determine how the group prefers to receive information so that we can be most effective in our communications efforts with them.

So, it is clear that all groups have their own unique communications preferences. The group's stage of development can make things more complicated if we do not pay careful attention to it. Under standing and recognizing the four stages of group development makes us better communicators. The better we can become at pinpointing the stage of a group, the more effective we can be in communicating with them.

To determine how to most effectively communicate with a group, you have to consider both the preferred communications style of the group, (which is likely reflected in their primary reason for existing,) and the group's current stage of development. From there, you can adjust your communications style accordingly.

Let's examine a group situation that I am familiar with. It is a country club (group) with members who pay to socialize with each other and have use of the club's private swim, tennis, golf, exercise and dining facilities. Generally speaking, the members of this group all live in close proximity to each other, are in a similar socio-economic class, live in comparable homes, drive similarly priced cars, and have achieved the same level of career success. OK—you get it—they have a lot in common. Most groups do. The country club has been around for years, so this group is well developed and in the performing stage.

Here is a story that a friend of mine, Jim, told me regarding his experience in communicating to this country club. Jim, the newly elected treasurer of the group, needed to convey the club's financial situation at the next board meeting. His recommendation, based on the numbers, was that each member's monthly dues be increased. Oh yeah—let me mention that Jim is a serious and detail-oriented attorney. He has a direct style, gets right to the point and is a man of few words. Based on what you have read about personality types, you get the picture (i.e. *think-first, speak-later; just-the-facts; head; and 5 o'clock sharp*). Wow, as you can see Jim meets all of the criteria for a reflective, factual, direct, logical and time-sensitive communicator.

To be effective in his message to this "fun-loving group" that has been around for years, however, it is imperative that Jim modify his style. He must adapt his natural type of communications to match the group's style so he can deliver his message in an effective manner. Remember this is a group that is not lacking for money, who values their image, and whose members stay involved to have fun. So how should Jim go about communicating to this group? Let's look at two scenarios—the first one is bad and the second one is good.

Jim says, "Alright, folks, let me make it real simple. We are faced with an annual deficit of $25,000 dollars this year at this club, and we are losing our edge. In order to balance our books, we need to increase each member's dues $1,200 per year. I make a motion that we approve my recommendation. Can I get a second?"

(As you might imagine, his direct style did not go over real well, and he immediately got push back.)

One club member immediately demanded a copy of the budget. "Where is all the money that we currently pay going? You know, I am already unhappy with the fact that our golf course is closed two days a week—and now this!"

Another member stated, "Well, I am disappointed too. One of our tennis courts requires serious work. It needs to be resurfaced and needs new nets. This is supposed to be an elite club. How much do we already pay for such maintenance, and why hasn't this already been done?"

Can you see what happened? Jim was direct, to the point, and spent no time "setting up" his presentation in a manner that would appeal to the club members. He used his natural communications style of *think-first, speak-later; just-the-facts, head;* and *5 o'clock-sharp* to share the message. Remember this group likes to talk things out (*speak-first, think-later*); focus on their image in the community and what could be (*big-picture*); have fun and build relationships (*heart*), have been together a long time (performing), and do not like to be pushed to make quick decisions (*5 o'clock-somewhere*).

Jim was communicating to a group, of which he is a member, that had a collective style exactly the opposite of his individual type. In addition, when presenting the message, Jim did not answer the "whys" and simply told them the "whats" which again worked in complete contrast to the way the country club group preferred receiving information.

Also, he failed to mention all the good things that had been accomplished at the club in recent months. Moreover, he did not emphasize that the increase in dues would likely be for a short period of time, and instead told them how much it would be for an entire year. So, because Jim left out this relevant information, the message to the members fell on deaf ears. They saw no benefit, and Jim failed in this first group communications attempt.

This situation could have been different. Jim could have recognized that his interest in facts, attention to details, and direct approach was not a style shared by this informal and relaxed group as described above. For the most part, this country club group (in the performing stage) was dynamic, big picture, relationship and entrepreneurial focused in nature. So, if Jim had deliberately moved outside his "direct and no frills" style, he might have presented in this manner. Notice the changes in the second scenario and how Jim meets the communications needs of the group. He says basically the same thing as before; however, he says it in a different way.

> *Jim says, "Thanks to all of you for being here tonight as we discuss an important issue that affects all of us at our top-notch country club. As you know, everything affects me the same as it does you. I want us to be able to talk this situation out and look at the big-picture implications for us. Remember it is all for one and one for all.*

> *One thing we all pride ourselves on here is having a beautiful and well kept, swim/tennis/golf facility that our families and friends can enjoy, and we can all be proud of. So you know, the club's cost for landscaping, security, and regular maintenance has increased a good bit in the past year.*

> *Since we all want to protect and preserve our country club—which also keeps our property values up—I would like to recommend a solution. I ask that we vote to increase our monthly dues to cover the increase in costs we are experiencing. This allows us to*

keep our club in great shape now and in the future and also protects our investment and community. It is likely that this increase will only be for a short period of time, but for now it something we really need to do.

So, if you value this club like I do, let's vote for this increase. The increase for each member would be $100 more per month. Again, approving this modest increase will ensure we remain an elite country club. Before I propose a vote—which we do not have to take at this meeting as it will give you all time to think through this—can I answer any questions? Do you have comments? Again, I want us to talk this through."

In this scenario, Jim adjusted his communications style to match the preferred style of this group. Furthermore, his presentation appealed to the interests of the group. He focused on the image of the country club and explained the "whys" to them, and not just the "whats." You see he talked about the fact they were all in this together (*heart* perspective). He offered them time to focus on the overall implications to the club (*big-picture*). He was open to them voting now or at a future meeting (*5 o'clock-somewhere*), and finally he shared that he wanted them to discuss what he was presenting (*speak-first, think-later*).

In addition, he approached the financial aspect of this discussion by talking about temporary price increases—which everyone can understand. And, he did this after he had made some preliminary points with valuable content. He only talked about how much more it would be per month—not per year. He did all of these things to meet the group's communications needs.

Jim adapted his communications and thus the overall message in this second scenario was quite successful. Effective group communications occurred as he adapted his "direct" style of communications to meet the group's "laid-back" type of communications.

There are many different types of groups. In addition, groups form and/or exist for many reasons. A group may be a family that gets together because they are blood relatives. A group may develop because people work together in the same office each day. Some groups are a collection of friends that sing in a choir together. On the other hand, groups consist of people who play golf together each weekend.

Some groups form to socialize, like the country club example. In addition, there are groups that form to advocate for a specific issue/ set of issues (AARP or political party). We can find educational groups (classes) and support groups (Overeaters Anonymous). Groups can be formal or informal in nature. Moreover, a group can last for a long period of time or a short duration of time.

The most important things to remember when communicating to groups are that they have generally been formed around a specific set of factors that they have in common. Just like an individual has a style he or she prefers in communications, similarly most groups have a default communications style as well. This style could be based on their interests, lifestyles, religious beliefs and more. Groups, like individuals, can never completely be a "this" or a "that" but definitely have a communications style they prefer. Our job is to figure out what the group's preferred style is and then adapt our individual style to it accordingly so we can be most effective.

So, whether you are talking to your family, teaching a class, making a sales pitch to a corporate board, or making a campaign speech, it is vital to realize that you are communicating to a group. It is also important to recognize that this group has an overall type of communications it has adopted. Be sure to take time to assess both the developmental stage of the group (described above) as well as their preferred style of communications. Finally, adapt your communications as required so that your message resonates with them. You need to talk the language that the group does.

Here are some things to consider when communicating to a group:

1. What is the purpose of the group?

2. What medium does the group like to use when communicating?

3. What is the message you want to communicate?

4. How long has the group been around?

5. Who are the key leaders in the group?

6. What kind of information does this group prefer to receive?

7. How does the group make its decisions?

If you think through these seven questions, you will be better prepared to deal with different types of groups. For instance, you would not present to the executives at an engineering firm the same way you would to a middle school PTA board, right? You see, all groups are unique because they are made up of—you guessed it—people. So, while there is no way to give a comprehensive analysis of how to approach every group, the guidelines as outlined in this chapter will help you become more successful in adapting your communications style to meet the overall group needs.

CHAPTER 13

Your Brand of Communications

We have established the fact that the *Everyone Is in Sales* philosophy means that we are all in communications in some fashion. With that said, there is one aspect of communications that we have yet to address. The subject is how to build our brand of communications. In this chapter we will define what a brand is, why it matters, and how we can better communicate our brand.

Let me be provide some clarity (Yes—you are right—this is one of the 5 C's we covered). Everyone has a brand. Brands are not merely reserved for large companies or for Hollywood stars. This is what many people

> *Your brand is not what you say it is, but is what others say it is.*

believe, and each of these entities do have a brand—but in reality so do you. The fact is—everyone has a brand. The question then is not *if* you have a brand (yes) but instead, *what* do you do with your brand?

How do you communicate your brand to the world? Simply said, your integrated (online/offline) communications create your brand. Also, your brand is not what *you* say it is, but is what *others* say it is. This means that your brand is defined by others, and that their perception of you defines your brand reality. It does not mean that their perception of the brand you communicate is correct—but it does mean it is their reality. Thus, it is quite important that you work deliberately to build your brand of communications in every aspect of your life.

Why wouldn't someone want to communicate their brand in a consistent (as noted in the 5 C's model) manner? Good question. Some people desire to communicate their brand correctly, but cannot see that they are "off base" in their communications efforts. For instance, think of a person who invades your personal space when talking. I have learned that these people do not intentionally make you uncomfortable—they just lack self awareness or don't know better.

The below model, known as the *Johari Window*, was developed by Luft and Ingham. It is a helpful tool to use in reviewing your brand of communications and overall style. Let's take a look at each of the four quadrants below and discuss what they mean.

Johari Window

	Known to self	Not known to self
Known to others	Public	Blind Spot
Not known to others	Private	Unknown

The top left quadrant of the window deals with communications that are "public" in nature. This means these are communications that are known to both you and to others. There are no surprises here. So, if you are an abrasive person, you know it—and others do as well. If you are a passionate person, you know it—and so do others. So in thinking about your brand, (remember this top left quadrant) consider communications and behavior that are readily known to both you/self and others.

The bottom left quadrant of the window addresses communications that are "private" in nature. These are things that are known to you/self but are unknown to others. For example, maybe you are incredibly shy and hate speaking in public. You had a bad public speaking experience in the past (nobody knows this but you), and thus you to refuse to speak at an event where you are being honored. Many people might take your refusal to speak as a sign of arrogance because they have misinterpreted your brand. Why? You know the reason you are not able to speak, but others do not know it—thus this area is deemed "private." So, miscommunications occur. As you build your brand, you must carefully think about this quadrant. It is quite important, and as communicators everything we say/write or do *not* say/write plays a role in defining our brand of communications.

The bottom right quadrant is referred to as "unknown." These are things we all speculate about but do not have the answers to. Neither you nor others know what your life will look like in five years. So this quadrant is referred to as a "future, mystery, or God-type" thing. It is not in our area of control. It is unknown to all, and only time will reveal.

And finally, there is the top right quadrant that plays a vital role in your overall brand of communications. This category is referred to as the "blind spot." The blind spot is something that is known to others but is not known to you/self. This quadrant of the window provides a huge growth opportunity for our communications and brand development.

131

If you think about this entire book, I have stressed that the only way to improve in our communications is to work hard at improving our skills. But, how do we do that? First, we must avoid operating "blindly" or in the dark. How do we do this? One way is to obtain feedback from trusted confidants who live, work and play around us. If we can obtain such valuable feedback from others—who we trust—and improve our skills, why wouldn't we want to do that? The answers are pride, ignorance, complacency, stubbornness and/or embarrassment.

Let me see if this will help you. People already know your blind spot. I promise that they already know what you need to work on, and these people—who you will ask—like you anyway. Although their feedback may be new to you—it will not be a surprise to them. So here is a question to consider as you embrace the *Everyone Is in Sales* mindset. Will you seek out those you trust and ask them to help you with your blind spot as it relates to your brand of communications? Here are some examples.

Could it be you talk over/interrupt people when talking to them? Could it be you always tell a story that tries to "one-up" what another person just told? Could it be that you are not an active listener? Could it be that your style is really loud and rubs people the wrong way? Could it be that you are too "wishy-washy" in your verbal commitments? Could it be that you are overly negative? As you can see the list is endless.

You may think that I am asking you to go out and have others point out your faults. Wrong! We all have plenty of strengths and weaknesses. The person you will be asking has plenty of their own blind spots as well that you could help them with. We are all in the same boat. We are all human. We all have faults. The difference is some people seek to learn their faults and improve, and others—for whatever reason—do not. Staying the same is not a possibility. You are either growing and moving forward, or you are slowly declining and moving backward.

Thus, the only real "fault" is doing nothing at all. For example, there is something you need to improve and can improve, yet you do nothing—and make no effort to get better. People who embrace the *Everyone Is in Sales* philosophy seek to uncover and improve their blind spot and see it as an opportunity to grow their brand of communications. Once you become aware of a blind spot, it becomes something you can work to improve. And, over time, this blind spot will diminish and oftentimes becomes an area of strength.

Here are a couple more blind-spot examples in regard to your brand of communications. What if you view your style as being diplomatic and relaxed, yet everyone around you, if asked, would define it as being argumentative and aggressive? What if you think of yourself as a person who is great at delegating things, but others define your style as one that seeks to micromanage every part of a project?

A blind spot in your communications style will hinder your brand. It is as simple as that. Think of your blind spot this way: If you are backing your car out of your driveway and cannot see that you are about to run into your mailbox, you are experiencing a blind spot. However, what is interesting is that you can clearly see your neighbors in the road, and, if you ask them, they can help you navigate the area you cannot see (blind spot).

However, maybe due to pride or overconfidence, you do not ask for their help, and instead smash into the mailbox. Was this a surprise to them? Of course not. They saw it coming the entire time although you could not. Again, if you would have simply asked for help, you could have avoided the mailbox.

So maybe you don't like to have others help you. OK, fine. But, my point is, which is more embarrassing; asking for guidance (proactive) or running into a mailbox (reactive)? I think you see the point. The same concept holds true in every aspect of life. In short, this is what the blind spot is all about. If you want to grow and improve your brand of communications—in this rapidly changing world—become aware of and improve your blind spot.

So you now understand that everyone has a brand, and that it is defined by others. In addition, you know that your brand of communications can improve, but requires learning where you are weak, and then embracing and improving your blind spot.

But, what is a brand and how does it affect our communications? First, building a strong, trustworthy, and reliable brand takes time, effort and commitment. Sorry—no shortcuts. This hard work pays off by creating something referred to as *brand loyalty*. Brand loyalty is one of the most valuable assets any individual can have. This is when you hear someone being described with expressions like: "I would trust that guy with the keys to my house." Or, "Wow, does he ever walk the talk." Or, "John's word is his bond. You can take it to the bank."

To help simplify this subject, I have developed an acronym that can help you better understand and examine the subject of a brand. It will also guide you as you go about building and communicating your brand.

Your brand can be considered the "B" Barometer reading of your "R" Reputation, "A" Attributes, "N" Name, and "D" Distinctiveness. So let's look at each one of them.

- **B is for *barometer reading.***

A barometer is a measuring device, and a brand is something that is measured. It is shorthand for what others think of your brand when asked to define it. Since your brand of communications is going to be measured, be sure that all of your communications are in alignment (remember the 5 C's).

- **R is for *reputation.***

Your reputation is established over time. It comes in large part from how you communicate with others. Over time, people observe what it is that you stand for, care about and believe in. They do this by reviewing the issues that matter to you and observing the life you lead. For example, if you spend time volunteering and serving others, you gain a reputation as a person of humble integrity. In contrast, if your style—whether talking to parents of the kids on the soccer team you coach or to the board of directors of a corporation—is not authentic, your brand will be seen as lacking integrity and your message will be discounted.

- **A is for *attributes*.**

The attributes you convey are noticed by others as they watch how you interact with the world around you. Are you strong minded, or do your actions and words indicate tentativeness? Do you draw others into your circle of influence, or is your communications style exclusive in nature? Are the words and tone of your communications kind, or do you invite apprehension? Remember that each and every time you communicate a message, it helps others define your attributes.

- **N is for *name*.**

Is your name well known within your professional, personal, and community circles? Do others recognize who you are, what matters to you, and what you stand for? Do they think of you when they are seeking guidance in your areas of expertise? Be certain that your name is clearly communicated and associated with the things that matter most to you in life. There is a song called *Remember the Name* by the artist Fort Minor that makes a good point: in your brand of communications, it is all about people remembering your name. The song says, "It is 10 percent luck, 20 percent skill, 15 percent concentrated power of will, 5 percent pleasure, 50 percent pain...and a 100 percent reason to remember the name."

This is true: your name, if remembered for good things, truly impacts your brand of communications. You can work hard to display your reputation, attribute and name, but unless you are distinctive, few may notice.

- **D is for *distinctiveness*.**

Your distinctiveness involves your willingness to be creative in the approach, means, mediums and methods of your communications. You must find a way to make yourself stand out from others. You need to develop unique insights. You need to shake things up by challenging people to see things—including yourself—in a new light. If you succeed at being distinctive, people will want to communicate with you and embrace your brand, and will find new ways to understand you, themselves, and the world around them.

I developed this acronym for the word brand after reading countless articles and books in the popular and academic circles. To me, this definition nails it. If you will embrace this brand acronym as you communicate, you will be more successful in all of your endeavors.

With this information, you can begin to determine the ways you want to purposefully grow, change, re-frame, promote, and strengthen your current brand of communications. Remember, we all have a brand—our choice is what to do with it. And, as we close this chapter let me leave you with this…

There are three types of people in the world; those who make things happen, those who watch things happen, and those who wonder what happened. Become a "make things happen" person and grow your own unique and powerful brand of communications. This is what the *Everyone Is in Sales* mindset is all about.

CHAPTER 14

Everyone Is in Sales = the New Face of Communications

Well, we have come full circle. It has been a fun journey and one that I hope you have enjoyed as much as I have. Many of the concepts in this book will stand the test of time. You see, I did not seek to write a book that was merely a fad. Nor, did I want to write a "flavor of the month" book. I sought steak, not sizzle.

My goal was to explain sales in a new way. I wanted to challenge our conventional concept of sales. I am confident that we have done just that. My hope is that that you will you use this book (over time) as a tool to help you—no matter what you do for a living or what stage of life you are in. It blends the best of the traditional with the new, and the best of the academic realm with the professional sector. It appeals to all age groups. This was my goal, and I am pleased with the result.

As I mentioned before, we live in a rapidly moving and changing world that will continue to evolve even more quickly in the years ahead. So our choice of how to respond to the change is

137

simple. We can go live in a cave somewhere, or we can decide to embrace this new world in a proactive manner.

The key to all of this is that our relationships (online and offline) are integrated in nature and built on solid two-way communications. Remember that "*s*" (plural) added to the end of *communication* means a lot. So, never forget that communications center on the human being—never on the technology. The technology will change, but humans will not—we will always have basic needs (as we have explored in this book).

> *We can go live in a cave somewhere, or we can decide to embrace this new world in a proactive manner.*

As you may recall, I began this book by reframing the word *sales* from a traditional, "have I got a deal for you," and gimmicky sales pitch to a new definition. A better definition. My goal was to explain that sales (as defined in this book) are simply communications at the highest, best and most effective level. We *are* all in communications. People who understand the topics, models, stories, tools and more—that have been covered in this book—can truly embrace the *Everyone Is in Sales* mindset.

Your concept of sales has been broadened, refocused and reframed to encompass the full range of the communications process. Utilizing new methods such as the *5 Why's Communications* model, the *Adaptive Communications* model, and the *5 C's Communications* model we have illustrated tangible take-aways that you can apply to your life. In addition, we have provided ways to understand both your own and others' (individuals' and groups') communications styles. We have explained how to adapt your style to find common ground with others and communicate more successfully.

I challenge you to consider your degree of competence in communications as you work on these concepts. The goal is to recognize where you are today in order to determine where you seek to go in the future. The four stages of communications, developed by Noel Burch, are listed below. As you review them, consider your own behavior patterns, then determine where you are and envision where you want to be.

1. The Unconsciously Incompetent Communicator

We must first look at stage one, the *unconsciously incompetent* communicator. When a person is in this stage, they are oblivious to what they do not know. In other words, they are not even aware of what they know or do not know. This is a dangerous place to be. Many persons in this stage think they know more than they actually do and tend to overestimate their overall skills and abilities as communicators.

2. The Consciously Incompetent Communicator

In the second stage, a person is *consciously incompetent* in their communications. This means a person is totally aware of how much they do not know. The good thing about this stage is that they are not in denial—they know they need to improve, and are not over-confident. To improve, however, the person must learn new things to become competent in the areas of their communications where they are lacking.

3. The Consciously Competent Communicator

The third stage is when a person is a *consciously competent* communicator. In this level, a person is cognizant of what they are doing well as communicators, and they are effective at what they do. So think of a person in this stage as one that is committed to "lifelong learning." They are good yet realize they must continue growing in order to keep improving.

4. The Unconsciously Competent Communicator

The final stage of communications is stage four. This is when a person is *unconsciously competent* in their communications. Persons that have evolved to this stage, the highest level of development, are so competent in their communications that they no longer have to think about them. Simply said, their competence is ingrained in their DNA and comes as second nature.

As we near the end of this book, I want to you to reflect—now and in the months ahead—upon your current stage of communications competence and on where you want to be. Here is a good way to remember the four stages.

Take a moment and reflect on different times in your life that you were driving a car.

- In your earliest stage, you were *unconsciously incompetent*. This means you did not realize how little you knew about driving. You were simply unaware of your lack of knowledge, skills, ability and experience.

- After you had driven for a year, however, this changed and you became *consciously incompetent.* You realized—usually after a speeding ticket or fender bender—how much you did not know about driving and how much improvement you needed.

- After driving for five years, you likely moved into the *consciously competent* stage. At this point, you became a good driver and also had experience to draw from. However, to a certain degree, you still had to think about what you were doing to drive in a safe manner.

- The fourth stage, being an *unconsciously competent* driver, likely occurred after you had driven for decades. Simply said, you couldn't remember a time when you were not driving—as it had become second nature to you. You could skillfully operate an automobile without even thinking about it.

I provide these examples about driving as they are something many of us can relate to. The further you move towards stage four whether as a driver or as an expert communicator (be sure to take the EIS assessment in the appendix), the more successful, efficient, and effective you will become in your communications.

As I reiterated throughout this book, there is great power in using adaptive communications. This model, which you will want to refer to many times, will help you better understand yourself and others—and both your and their unique worldview and motivations. When you can successfully tailor your style to match that of others, you are positioned to accomplish your goal of effective communications or yes...sales.

Once you are able to find this "point of compatibility" with them, you are poised to be deliberate, intentional, and purposeful in whatever medium of communications you choose. At this point, true communications can occur. When we utilize adaptive communications, our face-to-face interactions are most successful. In addition, our written collaboration flourishes and our social media and online communications are most productive as well.

Integrating the concepts taught in this book into your everyday life will help you become a better communicator. Whether you are communicating "one-on-one" or "one-to-a-group," whether you are offline or online, whether you are establishing your brand or simply talking to a friend, the *Everyone Is in Sales* philosophy is the new face of communications.

You picked this book up thinking it would be just "one more book" about traditional sales. You were worried where I was going with this. You thought, "This is a clever title, but what is the catch?"

You were worried about the "monster at the end of the book" that we call—*sales*. By the way, special thanks to my friends at *Sesame Street* for the idea. But, the monster at the end of the book turned out to be, just like Grover in the *Sesame Street* book, no monster at all. You see sales = communications. Nothing more and nothing less. You just have to shift your mindset and get past the "I'm not in sales" thinking. This is what we have accomplished in this book.

In short, be the best "salesperson" you can be. That's right—I said *salesperson*. You are not "turned off" by the word any more— you now see it in a new light. You see *sales* as it should be—as communications.

Embracing the *Everyone Is in Sales* philosophy will make you a better leader, co-worker, spouse, parent and friend. The end result is you will achieve your goals while helping others accomplish theirs as well. We all win, individuals thrive, organizations progress, and communities prosper.

Everyone Is in Sales—and yes, that means you—and our world is better for it.

Appendix:
Everyone Is in Sales checklist

To help you determine how good of a communicator you are, here are some questions for you to consider. Think of this as your checklist to evaluate where you stand in your communications.

Below you will find nine descriptions of strong communicators who embrace the *Everyone Is in Sales (EIS)* philosophy.

For every EIS person description you identify with, give yourself a point. In contrast, if you do *not* identify with the EIS description, do *not* give yourself a point. So you can get as many as nine points and as few as zero points.

1. The EIS person operates with the highest degree of ethics and integrity in all aspects of life. All communications efforts are focused on meeting the needs of all parties.

2. The EIS person seeks to engage in meaningful conversations with other people and listens to them in an active manner.

3. The EIS person is creative and consistent in their communications. They are able to integrate these communications in both their online and offline worlds.

4. The EIS person is authentic and does not take themselves too seriously. They are likeable, approachable, down to earth and helpful.

5. The EIS person has an unyielding belief in what they communicate to others. These people "walk the talk" and do what they say they are going to do.

6. The EIS person understands there are no shortcuts or tricks in communications, and all relationships are built on trust.

7. The EIS person is a well-rounded communicator in all parts of life. This person writes well, speaks well and is a good listener.

8. The EIS person strives to improve daily in their communications. No matter what level they are at (great, good or bad), they see room to grow their communications skills.

9. The EIS person is committed to learning both their own and other people's styles of communications in a deeper way to become better communicators.

The scoring breakdown is as follows: 7-9 points = superstar/EIS communicator. 4-6 points = above average/EIS communicator; below 4 points = needs improvement/EIS communicator.

1.___ 2. ___ 3. ___ 4. ___ 5. ___ 6. ___ 7. ___ 8. ___ 9. ___

About the Author

Ryan T. Sauers is President/Owner of Sauers Consulting Strategies. Ryan spent nearly 20 years leading visual communications companies (such as printing and promotional product ones) before launching his own consulting firm. Sauers is currently working on a Doctoral degree in Organizational Leadership and has a Master's degree in Organizational Leadership. He is a Certified Myers Briggs Type Indicator (MBTI) Practitioner and a CME (Certified Marketing Executive) through Sales Marketing Executives International. He uses his academic knowledge and professional experience to help organizations grow in new ways.

Ryan is both Director and Founding member of the Certified Marketing & Sales Professionals Association. He writes feature articles in a variety of media outlets on topics such as sales, marketing, communications, and leadership as well as a recurring article in a regional publication. Sauers is a regular speaker and presenter at a number of different industry conferences and events.

He spends time helping integrate the diverse worlds of new technology such as social media with traditional media such as printing and promotional products. Sauers is often referred to as a thought leader in both communications realms. He authors a blog which helps organizations position themselves in the most effective manner. Sauers is a university professor and consultant. He has an amazing wife and three wonderful daughters. To talk further, visit ryansauers.com or @ryansauers or facebook.com/sauersconsulting

pg 14 - the 5 whys
- example pg 15

Made in the USA
Charleston, SC
02 April 2013